Are you ready for an Outstanding Career?

This book is for you if...

- Your career is so important to you; it defines the very essence of who you are.
- You are highly driven and aspirational but work is wearing you out.
- You expect your career to be meaningful and you're struggling to make it so.
- Your career has lost its way and is going nowhere.
- You're at a loss to know what is involved in building an outstanding career.
- You are bored and frustrated with your job.
- You know you have so much more to give but you're not sure how.
- You feel your career is not playing to your strengths.
- You want a career that provides more influence and impact.
- You're not getting noticed for projects or promotion.
- Your career is lacking passion and energy.
- Everyone around you is overtaking you.
- You feel lost and in need of direction.

Reading 'How to have an outstanding career' will give you the power to change your life and become the person you've always dreamed of being.

D1649456

What people are saying about Susan

Susan Scott has vast experience as a practising psychologist working in the UK and internationally. She has an intense curiosity that has opened her mind to the detailed requirements of her clients. This enables her to respond to their actual needs rather than imposing some dogma of little relevance. Susan lives and breathes the psychology of human endeavour, understanding the nuances of human development where one size doesn't fit all, and individuals need individual understanding, attention and the right advice. Susan's interest in the requirements of the young, and the influences of their career development, goes back many years, yet is right up to date, embracing the rapidly changing environment that confronts the young professionals today. Her insights into their needs and her understanding of the hazards they face and how to avoid them, or use them to advantage, are of enormous value, not only to the young, but to anyone determined to grow and develop a career.
Professor Derek Mowbray, Chairman, Wellbeing and Performance Group

I was having real trouble taking on too much at work and never saying no. I knew a restructure was coming up and I was desperate to show senior management how needed I was for the organisation. It all came to a head during a particularly busy period. I had been running on adrenaline for so long and almost suddenly it all ran out. I felt exhausted and like I couldn't take one more thing on. I spoke to Susan and she really helped me. Susan has an amazing style of being direct but also incredibly supportive. She coached me to understand what was happening and how to take back control again.
Campaigns Manager, Charity Sector

I was managing a difficult project with a difficult manager with a lot of big stressful events happening at the same time in my personal life. I ended up burning out which really affected me emotionally. Susan supported me and helped me with the coping mechanisms to recover. I now understand the triggers better and how to cope better. Susan's experience and knowledge means that she understands what's happening physically and mentally when you're stressed. I'm sure it was this combination that helped me recover much faster.
Product Manager, Financial Services

I've been in my industry for many years and knew I was an experienced professional, yet I had real problems with self-esteem. I would read into feedback and always find the negative angle and I'd overthink any kind of constructive criticism. It would have a knock on impact on my home life with me feeling stressed and waking up in the night to go over it. Susan helped me immensely - she worked with me to try and get in the mind set of my colleagues so I could understand more what they were saying to me. Susan has this knack of getting to the root of the problem. She's extremely solutions focussed. I trust Susan completely and would highly recommend her!
Management Consultant

I can't praise Susan highly enough – she is friendly and incredibly knowledgeable and really supports you. Everything is so well explained by Susan and the advice she gives is priceless. She always kept me focused on what I wanted to eventually achieve and when things are tough she helps me to see that a difficult situation is solvable rather than a crisis.
HR Advisor, Information Technology

Susan is a natural speaker and a true inspiration. Her energy and passion is infectious as she shares her wealth of knowledge and experience through her many examples and stories. A highly worthwhile investment for my company and myself.
Lawyer, Commercial Law

I've been lucky in my career to have risen up the ranks very quickly but this left me feeling incredibly guilty. I convinced myself that I had no credibility and stopped asking questions which impacted my work. Just understanding that I was experiencing Imposter Syndrome and that it was quite common was such a help. Susan helped me to look constructively at myself. I have regular sessions with her to keep me on track and I don't know what I'd do without her.
Digital Communications, Venture Capital

I was getting to a stage in my career where I knew I needed to make a change (either in direction or specialise) and didn't know what to do. All I needed was someone to be able to talk through things with me – a sounding board – so I could order my thoughts. I met Susan on a workshop she ran. She helped me to understand who I was, what I had to offer, what each direction meant and mapped everything against the aspirations in my life. Susan doesn't give career or job advice – she gives life advice and I can't help but do whatever she recommends – it works!
Administrator, NHS Trust

To John, Lucy and Ysabel, who everyday inspire me through their love and support me in everything I do.

I'd be nothing without you.

About Susan Scott

Msc, FCIPD, FISMA, MABP, MBANT

Susan is a business psychologist, a nutritional therapist, a trainer, a consultant and a coach, as well as a public speaker and an author.

She has worked extensively in the Information Technology, Management Consultancy, Finance, Legal and Charity sectors and has designed and delivered major change management projects and management, leadership and wellbeing programmes for numerous private and public sector organisations across the UK, Europe, USA and Australasia.

Susan brings a blended mind and body approach to her work. She believes passionately that everyone, but in particular The Young Professional deserves to work in ways that foster their resilience, performance and careers. And because of her extensive experience in working within organisations, she is very aware of the need for all staff to understand and be able to demonstrate the value they bring to helping their employer meet its strategic business goals.

Susan has an MSc in Organisational Behaviour from the University of London, a Diploma in Nutritional Therapy (Distinction) from the Institute for Optimum Nutrition and is registered with The Nutritional Therapy Council.

She is a Fellow of the Chartered Institute of Personnel and Development and a Fellow of the International Stress Management Association. She is also a Principal Member of the Association for Business Psychology and a Member of the British Association of Applied Nutrition and Nutritional Therapy.

She is a past Chair of the Trustees of the International Stress Management Association (ISMA[UK]) and is the co-author of "The Manager's Role in Stress Prevention."

Learn more

This book is just the beginning of your journey to creating an outstanding career.

To help you further, I've created several Tips Leaflets, covering many of the topics in this book, including Optimising Your Energy and Preventing Burnout.

You can download them for free and keep up to date with more insights by visiting my website **www.youngprofs.net**

HOW TO HAVE AN OUTSTANDING CAREER

and become the person you've
always dreamed of being

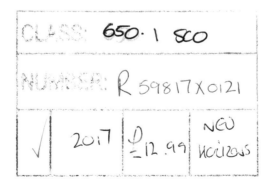

SUSAN SCOTT

Filament
Publishing

Published by
Filament Publishing Ltd
16 Croydon Road, Beddington, Croydon,
Surrey, CR0 4PA, United Kingdom.
Telephone +44 (0)20 8688 2598
www.filamentpublishing.com

ISBN 978-1-911425-71-7

Printed by IngramSpark.

Contents

Acknowledgements

I would like to thank a number of people for their inspiration and support with this book.

My mother, Jill, who instilled in me from an early age the importance of having a successful career.

Nicola Lewis and Jon Lassiter, whose many conversations whilst walking inspired me to write this book.

Anne Perret, for her support and encouragement during the writing process for the series of Young Professional books.

My publisher, Chris Day, from Filament Publishing, who believed in me and encouraged me all along the way – even if he did shock me at times!

My editor, Liz Sheppard-Jones, from Filament Publishing, whose energy and enthusiasm for the manuscript was the best boost to self-esteem a girl could ask for.

My designer, Clare Clarke, from Fusion3media, for turning 'words' into an art piece. Incredible talent.

Everyone, over the years and across the world, I have come into contact with in a work setting or talked about the world of work. All I know, I've learned from you.

To each of you, thank you.

"One can only know the best of oneself
through awareness of the best of other people."
Francois Cheng

Introduction

Why do you work?

Is it the money? Is it something to do to fill the time? Is it because it opens up opportunities to make friends and socialise? Or just maybe, is it because work provides you with the sense of purpose, meaning and self-respect that creates the identity you want to be defined by?

If so, and if you are between the age of 21 and 32, then you are a Young Professional for whom work is more than work. Your career defines the very essence of who you are.

You're in the early stages of your career, building a reputation based on your knowledge, skills, impact and influence.

How a career is viewed is changing. This is particularly the case for Young Professionals who expect their working lives to be meaningful. Traditionally, careers were like climbing a ladder, where with each new rung you had a new job with a bit more responsibility, and earned a bit more money; you just had to wait patiently for the vacancy to arise. It was about the job and because of this, most of the career books published still tell you how to find your next job.

The modern career is not about where you are on the ladder. It's about the personal meaning you get from the level of expertise you have and the influence and impact you have on the organisation you work for. It's these that will determine whether you get that promotion or dream job, not waiting in line.

You snooze - you lose

With this in mind, here's another question for you. What time is it? If you looked to your watch and told me the time, that's the wrong answer. The answer is that it's time to wake up.

As a Young Professional, you cannot afford to sleep your way through your working life. Making your career stand out is your responsibility and you need to take control of it. This means taking charge of how you develop your expertise, influence and impact within your current role. It's a competitive world, filled with aspirational high achievers, champing at the bit for the same dream job. You snooze, you lose - it's as simple as that.

As the poet Rumi wrote:

> *You were born with potential.*
> *You were born with goodness and trust.*
> *You were born with ideals and dreams.*
> *You were born with greatness.*
> *You were born with wings.*
> *You were not meant for crawling, so don't.*
> *You have wings.*
> *Learn to use them and fly.*

This book is the feathers in your wings. Use it and fly. If you want to get ahead, you need to feel confident and resilient, and to have passion and energy. This book will guide you on the journey to achieving this.

Why you need this book

- Are you highly ambitious?
- Is your career incredibly important to you?
- Are you at a loss to know what is involved in building a career?
- Are you feeling bored or frustrated with your job? Do you know you have more to give?
- Are you concerned because your career seems to be going nowhere?
- Are you frustrated because you're not using the skills you know you have?
- Does it appear as if everyone is overtaking you in your career?
- Do you feel lost, and need some direction?

If you have answered yes to any of these questions, then this book is for you.

The world of work is changing fast. Entering it can be an exhilarating experience and as a Young Professional, you bring many positive qualities including your motivation, the very latest knowledge and learning from your academic experiences and your desire to make a real difference. However, taking this talent and leveraging it into a meaningful career can be daunting.

This book will provide you with clues to what is important in careers today. It will prepare you to take action. What you learn and what you achieve from reading this book is still down to you, but if you let it, it has the capacity to open your eyes to:

- Who you are, what you value and what you do.
- The tools you need to tap the potential you have buried within.
- How to take charge of your career and propel yourself to success.
- How to work in a way that distinguishes you positively from other Young Professionals.
- Your purpose and aspirations.
- Where and how you can develop your knowledge, skills and competence.
- How to raise your performance, and in turn, heighten your visibility and reputation.

It can give you the capacity to cope with the challenging times you are very likely to experience throughout your career.

This book is designed primarily for Young Professionals, but it's also for everyone who wants to take some time to reflect on their careers and opportunities in a positive way; especially those that are willing to challenge themselves.

How to use this book:

This book may seem an easy read, but to get the most out of it, you'll need to apply some brain power. If you are tempted to just scan it then dip in and out, picking up the bits that are of interest to you, that is fine, so long as it's only a warm-up exercise.

If you really want to benefit from your purchase, you will need to read it cover to cover and work through it step by step, taking each part of the book in order. That's the best way to build your ultimate action plan and really understand what the topic is all about.

This will take time and commitment. Make sure you allocate time in your diary to work on it at least once a week. Momentum will build as you progress. Keep your mind open to possibilities and change. Embracing change is the only way to respond to the challenges your career will bring.

An outstanding career is a resilient career

You'll come across the words 'career resilience' a lot in this book. Here's why:

Your career is a long game. Short term manoeuvres may be important - but not as important as your long-term strategic thinking. To have a truly outstanding career, you need to be more than a flash in the pan. You need to build for durable, lasting success.

In a truly successful career, you will progress from one stage to the next, learning and developing as you go, achieving to your maximum potential. You'll move to the next stage when you're ready, with growing confidence and without crashing and burning. You'll become truly resilient, able to keep going in the face of short term setbacks and keep your eyes on the prize.

The book introduces you to the concept of a 'resilient career', then explains the Resilient Career Model. It provides you with case studies based on a real experiences, and tips on applying each element to create real career resilience.

Introducing 'brand you'

What will your career path look like? That's up to you, but knowing who you are now, and who you would like to become in the future is vital as you make the key decisions that will shape your future.

The book also takes a deeper look, not just at what you do but how and why you do it. We will define 'brand you': your values, your mission and your goals. As a result, you will gain a sense of your career journey as one you can control and direct. Whatever events you may face, and whatever unexpected turns the road may take, you will know who you are and where you are heading.

You'll also have a clearer sense of the strengths, tools and assets you can call upon on your career journey. This is what we will describe as your 'career capital.'

Your career capital

Career capital is like a bank account, but rather than containing money, the value comes from the collection of your personal qualities, skills, knowledge, training, experiences, achievements and relationships that you have to offer your employer and the broader marketplace.

Career capital is built up over the course of your career. With every new assignment you work on, every new skill you develop, every new bit of learning that takes place, you grow your career capital further.

We'll be defining that capital, considering the talents and abilities you begin with, the key competencies you need to add and the resources you'll acquire to become the best you can be in the workplace.

Take your time, open your mind

The aim of the book is to guide you in a very practical way towards creating your strategy for career success. To help you with this process, you'll find exercises in each part of the book for you to complete. Some are questionnaires, some tick boxes, and others require you to think for yourself and brainstorm. These can take you from understanding who you are and what you have to offer, to creating your career vision and the plan required to lead you to success.

Take your time, open up your mind, and work in a space that allows you to concentrate and think deeply. You are likely to find some exercises easier than others. If you are struggling with any at any time, do what you can do, then leave the book and do something completely different. During that time, your subconscious mind will be whirring away. This means that when you come back, you are likely to see things with a clearer perspective.

A fabulous picture of success

Think of every exercise as a piece in a jigsaw which, when eventually completed, will create a fabulous picture of success. As each part of the book closes, you will be given the opportunity to reflect on it.

Finally, although your career is your responsibility, the book does explore ways for you to involve your employer in your career development.

This book has it all, but it is down to you how you use it. The more you put in, the more you will get out. It's not a one-off activity, but a work-life journey. This book has the power to guide you through your whole career until the day you retire. The more you use it, the more successful you can be.

Part 1
Career resilience

2: What is career resilience?

- Do you want to build an outstanding career that leaves you energised and motivated?
- Do you want a career that's going somewhere?
- Do you want a career that defines who you are?
- Do you want a career where you use your strengths to the full?
- Do you want people to recognise you for the great job you do?
- Are you prepared to take ownership of and responsibility for your own development?
- And finally, but most importantly, do you want to be the best, without crashing and burning in the process?

If you've answered Yes to these questions, then it's time to start the journey.

The dictionary defines a career as 'the series of jobs, occupations and roles you may have over the course of your working life'. I want you to put this old hat way of defining a career completely out of your mind.

As a Young Professional, you are most likely intelligent, competitive, high achieving, and above all, aspirational. Your career is much more than a series of jobs or roles within your working life – it's the very core of you: your drive, your purpose, and above all, your identity. It reflects you as you are and as you wish to become.

Right now, it probably dominates your mind and is demonstrated in all you do. Your career is a representation of you and because of this, it is likely to be one of the most important things in your life.

However, achieving recognition and success needs to happen in a way that keeps you physically and mentally strong, energised and able to cope with all the challenges and demands that go with your work environment. Crash out or burn out and your career will never be what you had hoped it would be. Career resilience is the answer.

Career resilience is the capacity to apply yourself and create an outstanding career whilst maintaining your health and wellbeing.

Performance and wellbeing are inextricably entwined: you cannot perform well if you do not possess wellbeing. Wellbeing is one of those terms we're familiar with and think we understand, but it can be difficult to put into words. It includes mental and physical health but is also much, much more than this.

So what is wellbeing?

Wellbeing means:

- feeling vibrant, and physically and mentally able

- being healthily engaged in all you do - which means being careful about how much of 'you' you devote to your work

- working towards achieving the purpose and meaning you give your life

- feeling connected to people

- using all your capabilities so you feel a great sense of satisfaction and accomplishment as you deliver the best you can every day

- feeling confident and being aware of just how much you are developing and growing in strength and capability

- responding positively to change, instead of being fazed by it

- being able to challenge the status quo. You feel you are you; you're authentic and true to yourself

Wellbeing makes you productive, creative and attractive. You feel fantastic. You cope confidently with the ups and downs of working life. It's a life force… and if you're a Young Professional, it's a must.

What harms wellbeing?

However, wellbeing isn't an automatic right, it requires consciousness and effort. It ebbs and flows in strength depending on how life is at that point in time.

You need to be mindful of the things that drain wellbeing, such as:

- negative emotions
- self-defeating self-talk
- fragile self-esteem
- worries and anxiety
- lack of motivation
- procrastination
- stress
- a lack of purpose and meaning in your life

What fosters wellbeing?

Wellbeing is about you and it's your responsibility to develop it for you. No one else can do it for you, because what feeds your wellbeing will be specific to you. What works for you is determined by your unique personality, values, experiences and the purpose and meaning you place on your life.

Wellbeing can be divided into six themes: physical, mental, emotional, social, spiritual and career. Each will play its part in defining what wellbeing means to you.

1. **Physical wellbeing** – this includes good health and energy, physical energy from diet, exercise, sleep and overall mental and physical health.

2. **Mental wellbeing** – this includes self-confidence, the capacity to focus and concentrate, think clearly, remember well, be flexible and adaptive, manage conflict and avoid worry and anxiety.

Part

1

Career Resilience

3. **Emotional wellbeing** – this includes resilience, self-esteem, emotional intelligence, balance, belief in yourself, happiness, control of your emotions, thoughts, feelings and attitudes.

4. **Social wellbeing** – this includes positive relationships, feeling connected, supported, trusted, respected, assertive and confident.

5. **Spiritual wellbeing** – this includes a sense of meaning and purpose for life, passion, drive, fairness, and living in accordance with your values.

6. **Career wellbeing** – this includes career development, coaching, mentoring, role models, support, career path, self-awareness, life-long learning, using intellect, using competencies, using strengths, sense of progress, fulfilling and meaningful work, recognition, feedback, and engagement.

Think about what generates a sense of wellbeing in you. Try this activity.

Activity: Your life-force

Using the list above, identify what feeds your wellbeing. Think about examples of each as you're doing this.

Wellbeing themes	What feeds your wellbeing?
Physical	
Mental	
Emotional	
Social	
Spiritual	
Career	

If you are going to create career resilience, then it is important that you take on board the following critically important points. These are the five keys to career resilience.

🔑 **Key One** - your career is your responsibility

🔑 **Key Two** - you can't have it all now

🔑 **Key Three** - you need to know where you are going, otherwise you won't get there

🔑 **Key Four** - the road to success will be paved with challenges

🔑 **Key Five** - you need to ensure that your career is not at the expense of having a life

As these are so important, let's look in detail at how to turn each key.

The First Key To Career Resilience:
Your career is your responsibility.

Part

1

Career Resilience

Whatever your current role, you, and only you, are responsible for making your career the best it can be. Don't sit back and wait for the big rewards to come to you.

If you snooze, you'll lose because there'll be plenty of other Young Professionals with savvy and proactive mindsets ready to snap up and reap the rewards of the opportunities that materialise.

The reality is that your employer, even with the best of intentions, is ultimately only interested in what you can deliver and achieve in support of the organisation's goals. The more you do, the better for them. Yes, there is the chance that you'll be rewarded with extra responsibilities or a promotion, but this is not guaranteed. Your manager, even the very best, is primarily concerned with ensuring you deliver the results they need to shine themselves.

The psychological contract

There was a time in the distant past when you started a job with a new company and shared an unspoken understanding. This was the deal:

- you turned up promptly for work and did a good job

- in time you worked your way up that career ladder, filling someone else's shoes as they climbed onto a higher rung

- the company would pay for your training

- you had a job for life!

It is called the Psychological Contract. It is an unwritten expectation between employer and employee. The economic challenges of the last 25 years, as companies have downsized, delayered, merged and amalgamated, mean there are no more jobs for life. Now it's over to you to manage your career, not the company.

Taking responsibility is a scary thought. But it's not as lonely as it sounds if you take on board some of the suggestions laid out in this book.

You can plan your career journey, taking your place in the driver's seat. But you're not driving a car, you're driving a bus! In order to get there successfully, you will need room for lots of people and bags of equipment accompanying you on this journey. You can't do this in isolation.

To successfully take control of your career, you'll need to move your mindset.

FROM...	TO...
Waiting to be trained	Self-managed learning
Waiting to be told what to do	Using your initiative and doing what works best
Waiting quietly to be promoted	Being proactive so you're ready when the next promotion opportunity arises
Waiting for projects	Proposing projects that benefit you and your employer
Waiting to be motivated	Motivating yourself
Waiting for someone else to change processes	Proposing relevant and innovative improvements
Waiting for change to occur	Driving change
Doing the minimum	Going the extra mile
Waiting to be excited	Being passionate about what you do
Waiting to be inspired	Inspiring yourself and others
Waiting for things to fail	Persevering to make them successful
Waiting for others to learn	Helping everyone get better
Waiting for your boss to know the answers	Proposing your ideas
Waiting for a pay rise	Demonstrating your value – constantly

Part

1

Career Resilience

Get this firmly planted in your mindset and just do it (willingly!) That's how you will create the best opportunity to both succeed and to find fulfilment along the way.

The Second Key To Career Resilience:
You can't have it all now!

Your first day in the world of work is only the start of your journey. You have a lot to learn and do. Every day is progress along the route.

The career journey has a purpose. If you're patient and follow the process, you'll feel satisfied, optimistic and recognise success for what it is at that time... and that will make you feel so good.

As with any journey, you need to know where you are going. That doesn't mean knowing what company you want to be working for at each birthday. What it means is having a vision of what your professional life will eventually be, what sort of person you need to become to achieve that, and above all, understanding why, and what this will give you.

So - you might want to be a Marketing Director by the time you're 35, but what will this mean to you and your identity? That's what will focus and motivate you, not who you're going to work for next.

It's not about short-term wins

Taking a long-term view is incredibly important when considering your career. It can't be about short-term wins that in no time leave you deflated. It's about progressing step-by-step.

This is why you can't rely on your employer; they will have a short-term view for immediate gratification. A resilient career demands vision: a long-term goal with short-term targets to take you there in a realistic but challenging way. You will need to periodically assess how you're progressing and energise yourself by recognising what you have achieved so far.

Whatever you do, don't start looking for the next job as soon as you have started a new one. It will leave you frustrated, despondent and at risk of burning out. You come to a new job with innate talents and some skills, but during your time in that job, you'll need to build on those skills and acquire new ones. These will raise your influence and impact further.

Your career is a continuous process. It is one in which you learn, you grow in confidence and self-esteem, form relationships and gradually develop an identity. This takes time.

Along the way, you also need to develop the skills of self-awareness. How can you truly know what you want if you don't know who you are?

The three stages of your career

Thinking of your career as a continuous process prevents stagnation. You'll always be tuned in to how you can develop further. Your career journey within each role you take on requires you to:

- Develop your skills and knowledge.
- Grow your performance.
- Build successful relationships.
- Develop your influence and the impact you exert on the organisation.
- Learn about, and manoeuvre around a new level of formal and informal politics (and that's something we always underestimate; certainly, I did when I first started working).

The biggest challenge of all comes when you hit your early 30s. The demands of work mean you have so much to do that you are in danger of becoming too busy to develop your career.

As a Young Professional you will find yourself moving through various stages during your career. These can be characterised as follows:

Exploration Stage - when you are searching to find out what is out there and having initial ideas as to what you may be interested in

Experimentation Stage - when you begin to test these ideas. Try out various approaches to see what works for you and come to some conclusions about what you prefer or dislike

Development Stage - when you are growing and extending your capabilities in your chosen area, building your knowledge and extending your experience. In this stage you are also expected to show the results of your work and begin to grow your reputation

Part

1

Career Resilience

HOW TO HAVE AN OUTSTANDING CAREER

In practice, people with resilient careers are never solely in one stage. They are always to some extent aware of their involvement in all three stages, but to differing degrees, depending on where they are in their career at that point.

People in the very early stages of their career will mostly be in the Exploration Stage, with some limited time spent in the Experimentation Stage and very little in the Development Stage. As you progress through the Stages, the amount of time and effort you devote to each will change.

The following diagram illustrates this:

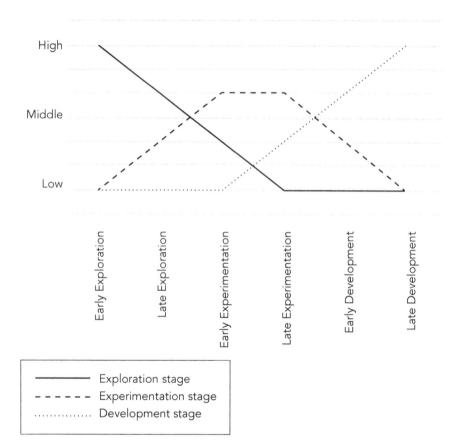

The Third Key To Career Resilience:
You need to know where you're going, otherwise you won't get there.

It's all about becoming who you want to be. Do you know who this is?

Maybe you did once upon a time, possibly when you were choosing your degree course, but thanks to the demands and craziness of the working environment, it's enough to get through the week now, so sadly those thoughts have long gone.

Having a purpose is central to your wellbeing.

> It drives you and focuses you.

> It gives meaning to your life which fires your passion.

> It provides a sense of reward which gives meaning to who you are.

> It builds your capacity to cope by focusing your mind on the end goal rather than the short-term annoyances and deviations that get in your way.

> It is your reason for existence and captures who you are and what you want to become.

Part
1

Career Resilience

You don't just have to have one purpose; you could have a variety of purposes that connect with different aspects of your life and are fulfilled at different times. But if you want to have a resilient career, then you must understand what you are working for.

Don't be tempted to confuse a purpose with a goal or a dream. The two are quite distinct.

A goal is fixed and measurable.

A purpose is clear but flexible. Because it's adaptable, you can deal with any challenges or changes in circumstances you meet on the way, such as a health issue or unexpected redundancy.

A dream lives comfortably in your head, popping up periodically to give you hope. But it isn't something you've committed yourself to.

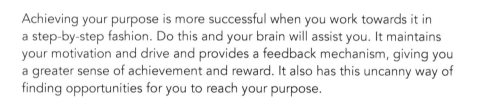

Achieving your purpose is more successful when you work towards it in a step-by-step fashion. Do this and your brain will assist you. It maintains your motivation and drive and provides a feedback mechanism, giving you a greater sense of achievement and reward. It also has this uncanny way of finding opportunities for you to reach your purpose.

Have you ever decided to buy a property and suddenly you see 'For Sale' signs everywhere? They haven't just appeared. They were always there, but your clever mind had filtered that 'irrelevant to life' information out.

And always reward yourself when you've successfully achieved the step you've been working on.

Activity: Your business card

You are going to create a business card with a difference.

This one states your purpose rather than your job title and contact details.

To do this, you need to understand who you are and what you want from your existence.

1. As a child, what did you want to do when you grew up? Write down everything – astronaut, nurse, doctor, cabin crew, work in a shoe-shop, drive a tractor… absolutely everything that you ever aspired to, from as far back as you can remember until you graduated. Perhaps they weren't all realistic. Perhaps over the years, they changed. But they do tell us about ourselves and our preferences.

2. If you can't remember ever having a dream job as a child, ask yourself what jobs you would still do now, if you didn't have to work for money and could do anything you wanted to do.

3. What do these jobs entail? What did you really love about each dream job? What purpose would they fulfil? What qualities could you have brought to each role? Record absolutely everything you can think of.

4. Now look for themes in what you have written. Is the common factor between doctor, nurse, teacher or work in a shoe shop because you love helping people? Did you want to be a tractor driver or fireman because you love machinery, or seeing the results of your work instantly?

5. Now create your business purpose card in the space below. Use the themes you identified to create a statement that summarises who you are and why you are here. This could be a motto, mission statement or an intention. Make it clear and snappy. Attach a logo. This could be something you design yourself or a picture or symbol you find. Make sure it's an image that represents who you are.

Part

1

Career Resilience

To inspire you, here's how the purpose cards of two very famous people might look:

To be a teacher. And to be known for inspiring my students to be more than they thought they could be.

Oprah Winfrey

To have fun in my journey through life and learn from my mistakes.

Sir Richard Branson

Activity: Retirement party

It's your retirement party and a very dear colleague who has known you for much of your working life is giving a speech. What would you like that person to be telling everyone about your work life? How close is what they will say to your purpose?

Part

1

Career Resilience

The Fourth Key To Career Resilience:
The road to success will be paved with challenges.

No matter where you live in the world, you will face challenges in developing your career. This is not just because of the demands on your time but also because you are operating in an ever-changing and complex world of work.

Since the 1980s, rapid technological change and globalisation have transformed the workplace. Uncertainty and change have become the only certainties, as employers focus on driving down costs and innovating across all aspects of their business activities.

Companies value people with transferable skills more than technical expertise, which can become outdated. They outsource and use short term contracts and other flexible methods of staffing to reduce costs and create organisational agility.

Your plan to create an outstanding career needs to factor in all of this change.

As a Young Professional who wishes to build and sustain a career, you need to be mindful of the obstacles you could encounter. You may not come across all of them, but with forward planning, when they arise, they won't necessarily derail your career.

As you face these challenges, what you learn and develop from the experience will enable you to add new skills, opening up a wider choice of opportunities.

Activity: Barriers to career success

1. Write down all the things you need to overcome or that could even derail you (your potential barriers) in developing the career you want.

2. Add anything else you have experienced in the past or anticipate experiencing in the future.

External Barriers

Lacking skills
Lacking essential qualifications
Insufficient experience
Too many demands
Not enough hours in the day
Unsupportive manager
Recent change in manager/senior leadership
Paid less than the market rate
No opportunities to progress within the company
Not privy to information
Market is too competitive
Problems with career history
Discrimination
Lacking support
No useful connections
Disability
Responsibilities outside work

Internal Barriers

Perfectionist
Fear of failure or rejection
Lacks courage
Lacks self-conviction
Introverted
Procrastinates
Takes on too much – can't say no
Lacks assertiveness skills
Low confidence
Low self-esteem
Overly cautious
Negative thinker - pessimist
Trouble concentrating
Finds it hard to focus
Resists change
Low energy levels
Suffers with stress, anxiety or depression
No motivation

3. What could you do to overcome them?

Your career barriers	What will help you

Part

1

Career Resilience

The Fifth Key To Career Resilience:
You need to ensure your career is not at the expense of having a life.

Life is for living, but as a Young Professional, careers can be completely and utterly absorbing.

The highest risk of burnout comes between the ages of 28 and 34. This is the time when you're throwing everything you possibly can at your career, but your position at work means you're maxed out with fulfilling the job role and meeting the demands from everyone and everywhere.

If your work is your whole life, your very identity, it makes it very difficult to distinguish between work and non-work time. Digital technology creates a 24/7 workplace and by the very nature of its accessibility, breaks down any boundaries there may be between work and non-work.

Frequently, when I run a resilience workshop, I ask what participants would like to get from the workshop and I hear 'how to achieve a better work-life balance'.

Work-life balance is changing

Work-life balance was a term developed in the 1980s. It describes a balance between the time you devote to work, and your leisure time. It was believed that a good balance makes you feel less stressed and more satisfied.

It was always a very individual thing. Some people feel strongly that you should be able to separate work and non-work time. Others actively blur the boundaries and blend the two with a mindset of 'always on'. Others may even ping-pong between them, depending on the work and non-work activities and challenges they are juggling.

Just like the dictionary definition of 'career', I believe the term 'work-life balance' is no longer relevant to today's competitive, high achieving Young Professionals. In fact, feeling that you're failing to get the balance between two entirely separate things right just piles more anxiety onto an already challenged state.

Life balance is the answer

In the twenty-first century, we need a term that is sympathetic to the reality of professional life. As a Young Professional, you spend a lot of your time in the workplace or engaged in work but you also need a term that captures time spent recovering.

I call this 'life balance'. You balance your life between activity and recovery rather than between work and home life.

Without allowing for recovery, you risk burnout. If you burn out, everything you aspired to from a young age will go up in smoke. Recovery from burnout is hard and it's difficult to get you back to where you left off.

How to avoid burnout

Take control of your life in a holistic way, rather than thinking of it in separate pieces. Modern communication technology, easily portable and with us 24/7, has made this an unhelpful model.

Balance 'doing' with 'recovering'. Take time to recharge your batteries. Energy is what fuels your life. So when you give out (by doing), you also need to recharge (recover).

If you're at work for long hours, try to ensure that some of this time is used as recovery time. This could be taking a walk outside at lunchtime, scheduling a ten-minute break every hour to do something less onerous and more pleasurable or organising your time so that it is not all knee-jerk reacting to events but some creative thinking time as well.

When not at work, make sure you are not caught up in 'mindless doing' or 'stressful doing'. Do some things that are pleasurable and absorb you, giving your mind a break from the work chatter in your head.

Socialising has an enormous impact on reducing stress hormone levels, so schedule time out with friends. Take on an activity that absorbs you, such as a sport, meditation, reading or gardening. Try to manage the time spent using digital technology, particularly in the late evening, as this has a profound effect on the quality of your sleep.

Part

1

Career Resilience

Take a reality check

The single most powerful thing you can do is to take a reality check. You can't 'have it all'. When it appears that others do, remember you are seeing only what they choose to show you. If you want to have everything and believe that this is possible, you set yourself an unbelievably high expectation and create a life in which you are bound to feel discontented and unhappy.

Life is not perfect. You can take this awareness a step further by identifying the desire that is the most important to you. Focus yourself on aspiring to achieve that, rather than trying for everything.

And you never know - sometimes the other things fall in line when that one thing works.

Activity: Recovery

This is your opportunity to identify your opportunities for recovery during your day.

1. In the left-hand column, list the themes of the activities that you do throughout the day (in and out of work). How does your day typically run?

2. In the right-hand column list the actions you take to recover.

3. Now consider what ideas do you have that could improve your life balance:

   a. How far do your recovery activities go towards recharging you? Stop and think how they make you feel and how they help your performance.

   b. What else could you do to minimise the negative effects of the activities in the left-hand column?

Activities	Recovery

Part

1

Career Resilience

Activity: Your reflections

Now is the time to reflect on your thoughts and the activities you have completed in this chapter.

Review the chapter in light of the following questions and record your answers below:

- What have you learned about yourself in this chapter?
- What do you need to change?
- What do you need to start doing that you have not done before?
- What other thoughts do you have?

3: The Career Resilience Model

Activity: Career Resilience questionnaire

1. Read the statements below and, thinking about yourself over the last three months, consider how much you agree with each statement.

2. Circle the number that most closely reflects your answer
    1 = Strongly disagree
    2 = Disagree
    3 = No strong feelings either way
    4 = Agree
    5 = Strongly agree

	Question	
1	I regularly spend time reflecting on who I am and what I do	1 2 3 4 5
2	I am in charge of how I feel	1 2 3 4 5
3	I take the time to relax and recover after a busy day at work	1 2 3 4 5
4	I take responsibility for developing my career	1 2 3 4 5
5	I look for ways to build good relationships with people	1 2 3 4 5
6	I am always on the lookout for opportunities to develop my career	1 2 3 4 5
7	I have a sense of purpose that guides my career	1 2 3 4 5
8	Even if I am overwhelmed by strong emotions, I try not to show it	1 2 3 4 5
9	I am able to prioritise my activities	1 2 3 4 5
10	I know what my strengths are and am able to use them in my daily work	1 2 3 4 5
11	I actively try to understand the other person's point of view	1 2 3 4 5
12	I have a large network of contacts	1 2 3 4 5
13	I know what drives me	1 2 3 4 5

14	I am aware when events affect my feelings	1 2 3 4 5
15	I usually feel physically and mentally energised	1 2 3 4 5
16	I track my progress and success on an on-going basis	1 2 3 4 5
17	I focus my full attention on others when I listen to them	1 2 3 4 5
18	I am curious and always ask lots of questions	1 2 3 4 5
19	I accept praise, compliments and feedback graciously	1 2 3 4 5
20	I can accept critical comments without becoming angry or upset	1 2 3 4 5
21	I eat well, sleep well and take regular exercise	1 2 3 4 5
22	I try to learn as much as I can from my current job	1 2 3 4 5
23	I find ways to become more visible	1 2 3 4 5
24	I embrace and drive change	1 2 3 4 5
25	I feel confident that I will succeed at what I do each day	1 2 3 4 5
26	I control my internal chatter	1 2 3 4 5

Part

1

Career Resilience

27	I am always able to focus and concentrate at work	1	2	3	4	5
28	I know the value of what I offer to my employer	1	2	3	4	5
29	I deal with conflict as soon as it occurs	1	2	3	4	5
30	I work hard to overcome the barriers I face in my career	1	2	3	4	5
31	I deserve my job	1	2	3	4	5
32	I look for the positive in most situations	1	2	3	4	5
33	I cope well with the pressures and demands I experience in my working day	1	2	3	4	5
34	I am willing to take the credit when it is offered	1	2	3	4	5
35	I understand and work around the political landscape where I work	1	2	3	4	5
36	I use a coach or mentor to help me and my career	1	2	3	4	5

Scoring chart

Now transpose your answers onto the scoring chart below.

1. Each box relates to a question. The box numbered 1 relates to Question 1 so put your score for question one in that box. The box with number 2 is for your answer to Question 2 and so on.

2. Add up each row and put the score in the final right-hand column.

What I think	Self-awareness	1	7	13	19	25	31	
	Self-control	2	8	14	20	26	32	
	Self-care	3	9	15	21	27	33	
What I do	My career capital	4	10	16	22	28	34	
	My reputation	5	11	17	23	29	35	
	My propeller	6	12	18	24	30	36	

How to score

If you score 25 and over for an element, you are demonstrating good career resilience for this item.

If you score less than 25 then you need to pay special attention to this when it is described in the book.

Part

1

Career Resilience

The Career Resilience Model

What you think and **what you do** provide the foundations to creating an outstanding career. If you are sleepwalking through your career, it is very likely that your work life is about mindless doing with very little thinking, particularly thinking about yourself.

A resilient career requires you to develop an awareness of who you are, what your emotional responses are and what impacts your personal wellbeing. Then you take responsibility and respond proactively to do what is required to develop and enhance your knowledge and reputation.

The Career Resilience Model outlines how to develop your capacity in a way that enhances your career and promotes your happiness, satisfaction and wellbeing.

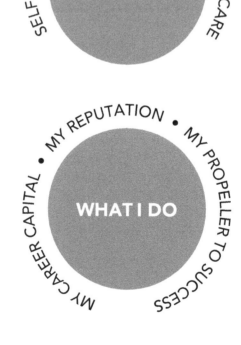

What I think:

1. **Self-awareness.** Sleepwalking through life means you give little time to considering who you are, but knowing who you are is a skill. It is about knowing what your talents and skills are, what you hold most dear to you and feel most strongly about and what drives you. This is one of the most important aspects of a resilient career. You cannot work in a vacuum. You have to interact with others and you stand little chance of doing this successfully unless you understand yourself.

2. **Self-control.** Part of our survival mechanism is to respond to threats immediately, with no time lag. To do this, we engage the part of the brain that draws on our experiences and habits. This response works much faster than logical thinking, in which you weigh up options. Reacting fast can get us into trouble. Instantly jumping to a negative opinion without considering other options, or getting upset or angry just because something similar made us do so in the past, doesn't make a positive impression on colleagues, or do anything for our reputation. Neither does it help our learning and development as a professional. Resilience means being in control. This comes from managing our emotions. It's all in the mind!

3. **Self-care.** The never-ending demands and challenges created by the workplace, as well by your internal chatter, make good self-care vital. Without it, you'll crash and burn. Stress, conflict and coming into contact with difficult characters all need to be considered in a more helpful way. This starts with understanding what stress does to you and how you respond when stressed. Then you can come into the moment and change the way you perceive the situation or person.

What I do:

1. **My career capital.** What do you have in your armoury to grow your career? This could include competences, knowledge, training, achievements, contacts and more.

2. **My reputation.** What's your personal brand? What makes you distinctive and absolutely compelling? How much influence and impact do you have? Your career hinges on your reputation as determined by the people you come into contact with, and this

Part

1

Career Resilience

can be tough when negotiating the slippery politics of the workplace which you'll inevitably encounter. Your reputation will make or break you because it's all about how people perceive you and how much they trust you.

3. **My propeller to success.** This is what ensures that your career flourishes and does not stagnate or falter as so many do. It's about distinguishing you from the crowd. You might consider yourself a high-achiever, but so do thousands of others. So what makes you better? There's a whole lot you can do that will distinguish you from the crowd and it doesn't matter how busy you are - if you want the rewards, you have to make the investment.

Activity: Your reflections

In the next chapter, we'll be looking more closely at the Career Resilience Model.

In preparation for this, take a moment to reflect on your thoughts and the activities you have completed in this chapter.

Review the chapter in light of the following questions and record your answers below:

- What have you learned about yourself in this chapter?
- What do you need to change?
- What do you need to start doing that you have not done before?
- What other thoughts do you have?

Part

1

Career Resilience

Part 2
What I think

4: Self-awareness

- Do you wonder why you can never stick by the decisions you make?
- Are you surprised by how people perceive you, positively or negatively?
- Do you find your self-esteem is easily knocked down?
- Do you have an inner critic in your head?
- Do you worry about trying something new?
- Are you convinced at times that someone will suss out that you're not good enough to be in this job?

If the answer to any of these is Yes, then you need to pay special attention to this chapter.

Self-awareness is the capacity to reflect on yourself and identify and understand the meaning of the different aspects that make up 'you'. These features include personality, thoughts, habits, motivations, feelings, emotions and behaviours. This is about asking yourself 'who am I?'

Understanding who you are is a critical activity when considering and developing your outstanding career as a Young Professional. Self-awareness provides you with clues on what might be holding you back. It creates choices that you wouldn't have known existed and the energy to take you on your journey.

Without it, you are vulnerable and travelling in the dark. Having an understanding of the dimensions that make up you enables you to read them in others and as a result, recognise the impact you could have on others. It's key to creating powerful relationships.

Activity: How self-aware are you?

On a scale of 1 to 10, where 1 is not at all and 10 is very aware, how much self-awareness do you possess?

Not at all								Very aware	
1	2	3	4	5	6	7	8	9	10

You must know everything about yourself if you are going to change and develop. That means not just what you think about yourself, but also what's hidden from you.

- **What do others know, that you don't know?**
- **What do you know that others don't know?**
- **What does no one know?**

What do others know, that you don't know?
These might be either pleasant to hear, or very difficult. Whether you agree with them or not, when it comes to reputation, perception is reality. If you're going to build a reputation, you need all the information you can get. The only way to know is to ask for feedback on your strengths and weaknesses, overall performance, effectiveness and potential.

Whether the response is positive or negative, what you learn will be enlightening and empowering. It provides the clues you need to build your action plan. Yes, it requires bravery, but take a moment to imagine what it would feel like to hear from someone senior in the company that they see you as a future leader.

What do you know that others don't know?
Some may be confidential matters which you choose to withhold. But there may be nuggets of gold that could help your career. If these include your career aspirations, or confidence wobbles that some training could overcome, you need to find a way to open up. By holding back, you are putting up your own barriers to creating an outstanding career.

What does no one know?
There will always be things that neither you nor anyone else knows. This is not unusual if you are in the very early stages of your career because you are still learning about yourself in the working world, and, hopefully, everyone you work with is getting to know you too. It requires a journey of discovery to find this out. This is where this book comes in!

Part

2

What I think

Case study

Joseph presented an update on his part of a project he had been working on and thought it had gone really well. So well, in fact, that he decided to go out and celebrate after work. He went back to the office feeling energised and excited for the future.

When he arrived his manager, who had been at the meeting, was at his desk looking rather serious. Surprisingly, he said nothing about the presentation. Joseph was perplexed. Why hadn't he said anything? As time went on, Joseph began to think more and more about his manager's silence. He began to wonder whether he hadn't done as well as he'd originally thought. The more he thought about it, the more his worries consumed him.

He began to dissect his work on the project. Maybe it wasn't good enough after all? Joseph knew there had been a few spelling mistakes in one report. He didn't always speak up at meetings and.... So it went on until he'd convinced himself he was hopeless. He left work that evening feeling low and despondent.

What was happening here?

People are busy. We can't expect them to praise us. It's more than likely Joseph did do a good job, but by reading into the situation something that was not there, he shattered his own self-esteem. If Joseph was looking for recognition, he would have been better asking his manager for feedback.

If it was praise he was after, it is not always readily forthcoming from people. Just because he wasn't praised on one occasion did not mean that he hadn't done a good job. Rather than allowing his runaway self-talk to convince him that he had failed, a good sense of his strengths and weaknesses would have made him more confident in the job he had done.

Top tips for self-awareness

- Reflect on your strengths and weaknesses regularly. How could you improve your strengths further and is there anything you could do, such as training, to improve on your weaknesses?
- Always have at the front of your mind what drives you. By knowing what your core values are, you will be more confident making decisions.
- Praise yourself for a good job done and do not let other people's inability to show appreciation affect you. Tell yourself daily how fabulous you are.
- Identify each evening, before retiring, three things that have gone well today that you are grateful for. This self-talk is a powerful way to raise self-esteem.
- Find ways to reduce worry and anxiety. This will grow your self-confidence. Stress management techniques such as mindfulness can help to calm the mind and help you to think clearly.
- If you ever doubt that you are worthy, stop and reflect on your successes. You will soon realise that you have every right to be where you are.
- Ask for feedback – it's the most powerful way to know what you didn't know!

Developing an accurate self-concept

Your self-concept is how you perceive yourself to be according to your natural talents, your learned skills and your drivers and motivators.

Having an in-depth understanding and appreciation of your strengths, weaknesses, fatal flaws and the personal qualities you value provides a platform for your career.

However, if you've ever sat down to reflect on what they actually are, then you'll know just how hard it is to capture and articulate this information – the mind has a tendency to go blank.

Strengths to build on
Strengths are the natural and learned capabilities you possess. They are your talents and skills and because you are good at them, you enjoy what you are doing and do a good job, which in turn makes you feel good about yourself.

This is why working with your strengths is energising, builds confidence and raises your profile. Strengths have the capacity to grow and develop further as you practice them and learn more ways to use them. This is why they hold an important position in developing your career.

Weaknesses to work on
Weakness are the capabilities you find hard to deliver. They take greater concentration, drain your energy and you don't actually do them particularly well. With effort or training, you could improve them but whenever you utilise these capabilities, you will not be performing at your best. That's why it's so important to understand what they are.

Fatal flaws to be aware of
Fatal flaws are more than just weaknesses. These are the things that you're utterly hopeless at and no matter how much training you undertake, you're unlikely ever to be able to do well.

Part

2

What I think

Activity: Your strengths, weaknesses and fatal flaws

What are your strengths, weaknesses and fatal flaws? You will need to dig deep to identify the underlying factors.

For example, recording that you have 'good people skills' does not tell you much. What is it that you are actually doing that makes you think you are good with people: is it intuition, being a good listener, motivational, firm?

This exercise can be difficult to do, particularly if you rarely give any thought to who you are.

You can learn what you need to know by considering:

STRENGTH	Your skills, values and knowledge Your past achievements: what you did that made them successful Things that come naturally to you What you do that gives you a real buzz Activities you would prioritise on your to-do list because you know you could do them easily
WEAKNESS	Your past failures: as honestly as possible, why do you think you failed? What you do that really lowers your mood or drains you
FATAL FLAW	Things you find exceptionally difficult Activities you would avoid at all cost

How does it make you feel when using each strength, weakness or fatal flaw? Record your answers below.

Strength	How does it make you feel?	How do you use it?
Weakness	How does it make you feel?	What can you do about it?
Fatal flaw	How does it make you feel using it?	What can you do about it?

Do the best you can for now and keep coming back to it. You'll have sparked off something in your mind that will let you know when you've done something worthy of labelling as a strength, weakness or fatal flaw. When this happens, pick up the book and record it.

Set aside time regularly to reflect on your strengths, weaknesses and fatal flaws. This needs to be an ongoing process, not least because as things change, different challenges emerge that require new skills. And of course, you're developing, so with that will come new strengths.

Part
2

What I think

Activity: Your preferences

A preference is a greater liking for one alternative over another.

Have a look at the following statements and highlight the word(s) that seem more like you. There are no right or wrong answers; all are characteristics that make up our personality.

Your preference

In general, when interacting with people, what is your preference?

Sociable and outgoing **or** Reserved and private?
Talk through with others **or** Think through yourself?
Talker **or** Listener?
Impartial **or** Sympathetic?
Leading **or** Supporting?
Assertive **or** Accommodating?
Individual **or** Blend in?
Directive **or** Collaborative?
Independent **or** Team worker?
Volatile **or** Calm?
Confident **or** Nervous?
Suspicious **or** Trusting?

In general, when working with information, what is your preference?

Facts **or** Ideas?
Write about it **or** Talk about it?
Detail **or** Blue sky thinking?
Hands-on and practical **or** Intellectual and theoretical?
Realistic **or** Fanciful?

Traditional **or** Contemporary?
Tried and tested **or** Try something new?
Conventional **or** Unconventional?
Questioning **or** Accepting?
Pessimistic **or** Optimistic?
Creator **or** Implementer?
Decide using logic **or** Decide using emotion?

In general, what is the way you prefer to work?

Get job done **or** Ensure people are content?
To get on with it **or** Analyse it?
Organised **or** Casual?
Planned and orderly **or** Let it emerge?
Routine **or** Variety?
Competitive **or** Non-competitive?
Driven **or** Laid back?
Early starting **or** Last minute?
Perfectionist **or** The minimum necessary?
Risk **or** Security?
Adventurous **or** Cautious?
Easily bored **or** Content with what you have?
Process-focussed **or** Results-focused?
Traditional employer **or** Entrepreneurial firm?
Conform **or** Rebel?
Autonomously **or** Directed?
Stable **or** Changing?

Part

2

What I think

Activity: 360 feedback

What do others know that you don't know? Work should not take place in a vacuum. It's in honest, even if harsh, feedback that you can learn about yourself and what you need to do to make progress in your career.

Now is the time to ask others about your strengths, weaknesses and fatal flaws.

1. Ask a variety of people at different levels in the organisation.

2. Preferably do this face to face – you'll be able to ask them to explain their reasoning which adds to the data you're gathering.

3. Listen to what they say. Do not interject or try to defend or justify yourself. Thank them for sparing the time to talk to you.

4. Record your findings below and identify how you will act on this new knowledge.

5. Remember that knowledge is power. Being a Young Professional is about reputation, so it is important to capture and address how others perceive you.

6. When people observe you inviting and acting on feedback, they'll feel good about working with you and more comfortable providing this on a regular basis, saving you the hassle of scheduling a special meeting.

What did they say?	How will you use this information?

What are my core values?

Activity: Your core values

What are the values that truly guide you and underpin what you think, say and do?

Take some time to read the list of values below. Place a tick in the tick column next to the values you really believe are important to you.

If you feel that an important value is missing, add it to the end of the list.

Values are guiding principles that work in your mind to inform your attitudes and behaviour. If you were cut in half like a stick of rock, they would be written right through you. This is not about what you would like to be like, what might be a 'nice-to-have' or 'ought to have' because your manager is like that or it 'will make you look good' – it is what is important to you, at the very core of you.

You will be most positive, committed and productive working within an organisation whose values and goals fit well with yours. Gaining a clear understanding of what your values are will help you make the best decisions possible and to work in accordance with your core beliefs.

If you're struggling with this activity, ask someone close to you to give you a few phrases or words that describe you and ask them to justify why. This may get you thinking and give you some clues.

Part
2

What I think

Value	Tick	Value	Tick	Value	Tick
Achievement		Fairness		Money	
Accountability		Faith		Novelty	
Advancement		Fame		Originality	
Adventure		Freedom		Patience	
Altruism		Friendship		Perfection	
Authority		Generosity		Positivity	
Autonomy		Goodness		Power	
Balance		Growth		Professionalism	
Belonging		Happiness		Recognition	
Challenge		Harmony		Reliability	
Change		Health		Reputation	
Commitment		Helpfulness		Responsibility	
Community		Honesty		Respect	
Compassion		Honour		Risk	
Competence		Humility		Security	
Competition		Humour		Selflessness	
Consideration		Inclusivity		Spirituality	
Cooperation		Independence		Status	
Courage		Individuality		Success	
Courtesy		Influence		Supportiveness	
Creativity		Innovation		Team spirit	
Curiosity		Integrity		Thoughtfulness	
Decisiveness		Justice		Trust	
Dependability		Kindness		Truth	
Determination		Knowledge		Uniqueness	
Dignity		Leadership		Unity	
Efficiency		Learning		Vision	
Empathy		Love		Wealth	
Empowerment		Loyalty		Wisdom	
Equality		Mastery		Work	
Expertise		Meaningful			
Ethics		work			

Review the values you have ticked and pick six values that absolutely represent who you are and write them below.

	Value
1.	
2.	
3.	
4.	
5.	
6.	

From the six you have selected, choose the three that are most important to you then identify the most important, second and third most important.

In the right-hand column define what this value means to you.

	Value	Definition
1.		
2.		
3.		

Part

2

What I think

Now record below why this is important to you. How do you live according to that value so people would recognise it in you? How does 'who you are' make a difference in your life?

What influence are your values having on your career?

For the next week, notice when you have lived according to your values.

Have your values written down somewhere close to you and review them when making big decisions. You will feel happier with a decision based on values and will be more likely to stick by that decision.

Some values will be with you for life. When you think back to important life decisions, you may recognise the part they played. Others may have come to the fore more recently because of an experience or life event.

At every stage of your career, operating in harmony with your values will give you strength and certainty. You'll achieve more and gain a deeper sense of satisfaction from what you do. When we align with our core values, we are at our most effective. This is how we make our career the best it can possibly be.

Your self-esteem

Self-esteem is the way you feel about yourself. It's the overall emotional evaluation of your sense of self-worth or personal value and it is founded on the beliefs you have about yourself.

Self-esteem is heavily influenced by the emotions you're experiencing at that time and by the impact you allow other people and situations to have on you. It's your own construction of reality.

Self-esteem is in your head and it isn't always founded on fact.

When self-esteem is healthy and robust, this is motivating and energising. High self-esteem will leave you feeling confident and positive about life. This in turn has a positive effect on your performance.

When self-esteem is low and unhealthy, it knocks you down, demotivates you and leaves you paranoid and thinking negatively about yourself. If you are stuck in this downward spiral of self-doubt, you are more likely to resist change and blame others, which will do nothing for your image.

Self-awareness plays a critical role in optimising self-esteem. It helps you see things as they really are, not what you imagine them to be in your head.

As a Young Professional, your self-esteem can be fragile

It takes quite a time in the work environment to grow a thick skin. An off-the-cuff comment by someone can create a dialogue in your head that becomes negative and self-deprecating, even though it may not be the reality.

Self-esteem grows out of praise, but you should not rely on others to provide it. You have to praise or reward yourself. After all, being a Young Professional is about taking responsibility for your career and this includes being responsible for telling yourself when you've done a good job. If you happen to receive praise or positive feedback from someone else, then you can take this as a bonus.

Part

2

What I think

Activity: To what extent do you rely on other people's perceptions of you to determine your self-esteem?

Here are some questions that point to low self-esteem. Answer them with a score of 1 to 4, where 1 is never, 2 is sometimes, 3 is frequently, 4 is almost always.

	1	2	3	4
1. Do you criticise yourself?				
2. Do you brush praise off when someone praises you?				
3. Do you worry about how others will view you?				
4. Do you need people to like you for you to feel valued?				
5. Do you look for the bad in others to make yourself feel better?				
6. Do you believe that talents are something you are born with?				
7. Do you consider people's worth is based on what you can see - job title, income, house, car, education, important friends?				
8. Do you consider yourself worthless when you compare yourself with others?				
9. Do you worry that others will pass off your achievements as theirs?				
10. Do you feel that you are always responsible when things do not go according to plan?				

	1	2	3	4
11. Do you spend your time worrying about the future and feeling fearful of what it might entail?				
12. Do you look back at your past actions and feel guilty for things you have done?				
Total				
Overall score				

Total up your answers.

If your total score is above 24, then that may indicate that you need to work on your self-esteem, because it may be hindering you and affecting your resilience.

Part

2

What I think

Here are some ways to develop your self-esteem:

- Forget perfection – life isn't perfect. We're all human. A mistake is a learning opportunity to help your development.
- Behave according to your values. It will ease your mind when you find yourself challenged, and make you feel more optimistic and resilient.
- If someone puts you down, deal with them in an assertive way by challenging them politely on what they have said.
- Find something challenging to do, inside or outside work. Reward yourself when you reach a new level of competence.
- Take regular exercise. Even if it's 'just' walking, it boosts endorphins in the brain – the happy hormones.
- Find opportunities to say 'thank you' to people. Eventually they will reciprocate.
- Forgive yourself for the mistakes you have made in your life and work. That was the past. Move forward on a new slate.

- Lose the 'I want everyone to like me' attitude. We're all different and there will always be someone we don't get along with.
- Find the good in yourself. Stop that negative self-talk. Positive people are more productive and more successful, which is hardly surprising when low self-esteem has such a negative impact on you.
- Be generous to others. The gratitude they show will give your self-worth a boost.
- Spend time with positive people. Avoid that Moaning Minnie in the office or the person who sees everything with doom and gloom – they'll drop your mood.
- Take compliments as a gift to your self-esteem. Don't feel embarrassed. Say, 'Thank you, it's kind of you to say that.' You will appear more confident by doing this, and more likely to receive more.
- Accept criticism with courtesy, then judge yourself with honesty later. What can you learn from it? Maybe it's based on one of your weaknesses, and hey, you have so many strengths.
- Acknowledge the good things you have done. Keep a note of these in a diary or smartphone and regularly read it – it will give you a boost when you feel low.

Self-confidence

Self-confidence is defined as 'how we feel, in general, about our ability to perform in roles, functions, tasks and situations'.

Feeling confident generates an expectation that you'll succeed. This is because self-confidence is a combination of self-esteem and self-efficacy. Self-esteem is our personal sense of self-worth and self-efficacy is the belief we have in our ability to successfully complete a task to a defined standard.

Low self-confidence can have a detrimental impact on your career. When your self-confidence takes a hit, you become anxious and want to avoid taking any risks that may expose you and rock your confidence further. This means you'll shy away from challenges that have the potential to be good learning and career development opportunities. Your talents won't then have the opportunity to develop further so your career will stagnate, preventing you from reaching your full potential.

Generating opportunities to grow your self-confidence is a must.

These can come from working on something that's challenging, but not impossible, where you have the opportunity to practice and make mistakes (providing you learn from them).

Encouragement and constructive feedback from your manager, colleague, mentor or other supportive people helps enormously, but you cannot rely on receiving this so it needs to come from you. This means you need to be self-aware, listen to yourself, trust yourself and provide yourself with an ongoing rhetoric of positive self-talk.

Activity: The ingredients of your self-confidence

Consider the following:

- What qualities do you have that generate confidence in yourself?
- Why do they?
- To what degree do you use these qualities in your work daily?
- How could you use them more to develop your capabilities and confidence further?

Part

2

What I think

Activity - Building self-confidence

What do you do when faced with something new?

Low confidence generates feelings of anxiety. Anxiety makes you worry that you won't be able to cope with something new that you are required to do. Does this happen to you?

If so, here is an activity to help the next time you are faced with a situation where you feel out of your depth.

Use this list of questions to help you get to the answers that will help you deal with it effectively and in a timely manner.

What is the situation? Describe it

What is happening? What can you see and hear?

How serious is it?

Do you need to do something? Must you?

What are other people doing or not doing?

How do you feel?

What emotions can you identify in others?

What previous experiences can you draw on?

How is this situation different from them? What are the implications?

What additional information do you need to obtain?

Where will you get it?

What alternative ways are there to deal with the situation?

Do you need to choose right now?

What is the worst that could happen?

Confidence tips:

- Don't try to do it all at once – take any changes steadily and step by step.
- Look for ways to expand your comfort zone by periodically taking a risk. This might be, for example, speaking up on something you don't agree with in a meeting.
- Don't expect everyone to like you. If you do, you won't develop anything but compromising skills.
- Give the impression through your body language and voice that you are confident – in time this will become the norm and you'll feel more confident.
- Give yourself permission to make a mistake. It's the best learning opportunity.
- Mix with confident people – it rubs off.
- Optimise your mental and physical wellbeing with a good diet and plenty of sleep and exercise to build your internal strength.
- Practice self-talk in the mirror. Rehearsing at least four times will help you when you come to do it for real.
- Keep a diary of your progress and score your self-confidence. There will still be some bad times if you've taken an unexpected knock, but you'll also be able to see where you've made progress.

Part

2

What I think

Imposter syndrome

There's one last topic I want to mention under the heading of self-confidence, because I hear Young Professionals express this so often. Do you feel a bit of a fraud at work: that one day people will wake up and realise that you don't actually know as much as you have led them to believe you do, and that you're not worthy to be in this job?

If you do, then this sense of self-doubt is called 'Impostor Syndrome'.

It's not unusual, especially amongst high achievers. It isn't necessarily a problem, unless it starts to inhibit you from putting yourself forward for something new and challenging.

Watch out though: people who experience Imposter Syndrome usually work much harder to demonstrate they are worthy of being in the position they hold. This puts you in danger of burning out.

Activity: What makes you feel like a fraud?

1. Think of three people at work you believe you have duped. This could be your manager, your HR department, a customer or a client.

2. Imagine you want to come clean, so you're going to tell each of them in turn why you are a fraud. How would the conversation go?

   a. What would you say to them?
   b. How would they respond to what you had to say?

3. Now…. who do you believe?

Activity: Your reflections

It is time again to reflect on your thoughts and the activities you have completed in this section.

Review the chapter in light of the following questions and record your answers below:

- What have you learned about yourself?
- What do you need to change?
- What do you need to start doing that you have not done before?
- What other thoughts do you have?

Part

2

What I think

5: Self-control

Have you ever:

- Been grumpy or irritable when under lots of pressure?
- Taken something personally that was said to you in jest?
- Been dismissive of or uncooperative with the new hire who robbed you of a promotion?
- Responded angrily to someone who didn't complete a task to your standards?
- Felt scared to speak up in a meeting?

If the answer to any of these is Yes, then you need to pay special attention to this chapter.

All these situations are expressions of emotion which may have a detrimental effect on how people perceive you. This could harm your reputation. Because of this, you require self-control.

Self-control is about taking control of your emotions and acting with restraint even when you're experiencing strong feelings. The ability to do this is one of the key contributing factors to a resilient career.

You will always experience emotions, sometimes powerful ones, but you are controlling them, and how they are expressed, rather than letting them control you.

Emotions are our spontaneous reactions to how we feel about our circumstances. They exert a powerful force on how we behave in response. The stronger the emotions are, the more they cloud our judgement about the situation.

As a Young Professional, your reputation is key

How do you feel when someone you're in contact with at work expresses resentment or petulance, or is grumpy and sulky, because of an event that has occurred? You'd probably feel pretty fed up with them. What about someone who expresses calmness, confidence, determination or curiosity despite experiencing the same situation? They're the ones you'd want to be around.

As a Young Professional, how you conduct and express yourself is going to be central to your success. Top performers are masters at controlling their emotions, and although we're all tempted at times to demonstrate how we're feeling, on the whole, being in control is more beneficial to us. Any act of negative behaviour will be noticed by people far more than all those wonderful academic qualifications and the previous experience that might have got you that job in the first place.

Positive emotions free up your mind

People are making judgements about you all the time. If you show all those you come into contact with that you don't take things personally, that you can cope with setbacks, can move on positively and manage changing situations optimistically, then it will be you they'll want to work with. You're the one who has an energising effect on those around you.

In addition to this, controlling your emotions also has a significant impact on your resilience. Positive emotions impact wellbeing and happiness as well as freeing up your mind to allow you to be more flexible and creative.

Controlling your emotions isn't easy when you feel passionately about something. If you find yourself in this situation, stop and reflect on the situation in a clear and considered manner. In so doing, recognise what you are feeling and the impact that expressing this feeling could have on yourself and others.

How could you express your emotion in a way that neither looks bad on you nor has a negative impact on others? By switching your response, you are expressing that emotion with a positive reaction rather than a knee-jerk negative reaction. This will be tough to begin with, but the more you do it, the easier it will become and the more uplifting it will be for you.

Case study

Lauren was a conscientious and successful account manager who worked as part of a large team. She liked to think she got on well with everyone, but there was one member of the team who really irritated her. This person just couldn't take blue-sky ideas for what they were - ideas. He always had to point out the worst-case scenario and nit-pick on every detail.

Lauren reached a point when every time she saw him, her stomach churned with the thought of his doom and gloom rhetoric. One day, the team was together in a planning meeting being run by the team's manager. The nit-picking began and in an instant, Lauren turned to him and told him to belt up. She followed up by asking why he always had to be so negative and telling him how everyone was tired of listening to him. For the rest of the meeting, Lauren ignored him.

Later that day, Lauren's manager called her aside to discuss Lauren's 'unacceptable behaviour', but Lauren couldn't see what the big problem was. As she saw it, this team member was a pain.

Part
2

What I think

What was happening here?

Lauren had lost control of her emotions and expressed her anger. If you are going to grow your reputation, you have to understand why a situation triggers something in you that may spark off a negative emotion. All of us can weaken at some time. But if we do, we have to apologise for our mistake.

Top tips to develop self-control

1. Take responsibility for your emotions – they have a profound effect on how people perceive you. Remember, you can only control yourself, not others.

2. Stop. Engage your brain. Think! Try to understand the emotion you are experiencing and why you feel that way. How can you get the best outcome from this situation? Whatever you do, don't over-analyse. If you do, you'll never get an answer or a better outcome.

3. Tune in to your self-talk – this is your inner voice chatting away to you in your head. What is it telling you? Is it positive or negative? Self-talk can have a big impact on the way you feel and what you do. If you talk constructively to yourself about the situation and why you want to respond the way you do, you will generate a better outcome for everyone. It's not the event that is making you feel like this, it is what you are telling yourself in your head. Only you can change that.

4. Try to reframe the situation. This is where you alter the event by highlighting the positive aspects. This has the advantage of cooling you down.

5. Solve problems before they get to you personally. That way you don't put yourself at risk of having a negative outburst.

6. Start each day by setting yourself positive intentions and at the end of each day, identify three things you have to be grateful for. Maybe someone smiled at you or your report was well received. This puts you in a more positive frame of mind, so eventually, you begin to think more positively.

Activity: Your emotional journey

Below is a list of emotions: positive emotions in the left-hand column and negative emotions in the right-hand column. Over the next three days, record with a tick on the chart each time you feel one of these emotions. When you experience an emotion, say to yourself: 'I feel….' then tick the relevant emotion.

DAILY TICK CHART							
Positive emotions	Day 1	Day 2	Day 3	**Negative emotions**	Day 1	Day 2	Day 3
Amused				Agitated			
Appreciative				Angry			
Capable				Ashamed			
Cheerful				Anxious			
Compassion				Bitter			
Confident				Disappointed			
Curious				Doubtful			
Determined				Embarrassed			
Energised				Envious			
Enthusiastic				Frustrated			
Excited				Guilty			
Fascinated				Hate			
Focused				Helpless			
Free				Irritated			
Friendly				Jealous			
Glad				Lonely			
Grateful				Miserable			
Happy				Nervous			
Inspired				Petulant			
Joyful				Resentful			
Motivated				Sad			
Passionate				Scared			
Proud				Selfish			
Relaxed				Superior			
Satisfied				Suspicious			
Thrilled				Worthless			

Other emotions   Other emotions

Part

2

What I think

At the end of each day, review your list.

- What is the balance – are there more positive or negative emotions?
- If you did react to any of them, what impact did they have on others?
- What could you have done to mitigate the negative emotions?
- At the end of the three days, how has your daily tally changed? Have you noticed a shift to more positive emotions as you have raise your consciousness about your emotional state?
- Think about the people you have responded to positively this week. How did that make you feel? That is the feeling you want all the time. It's uplifting, energising and contributes powerfully to your wellbeing, all of which will impact your career resilience.
- Get into the habit of reviewing your emotions at the end of each day.

Activity: Positive and Negative emotions

Think about the people you come into contact with who express positive emotions and negative emotions. This could be colleagues, managers, family, friends, partner.

In the left-hand column, record the names of the people who demonstrate positive emotions. What are their behaviours? How do they make you feel?

In the right-hand column, record the names of the people who demonstrate negative emotions. What are their behaviours? How do they make you feel?

What is this telling you? What could you do in response?

Name	Positive emotions, behaviours, feelings	Name	Negative emotions, behaviours, feelings

Part

2

What I think

Activity: An emotional situation

1. Describe a situation when you felt a really strong emotion.

   a. What was the situation?
   b. What did you see, hear and feel? Record it in so much detail that you feel the emotion again.
   c. How did the emotion impact on how you reacted?

2. Now ask yourself – was your interpretation of the situation correct? What proof do you have?

3. What could you have done that would have created a different outcome?

4. What impact would this have had on how people perceived you?

5. What have you learned about this situation?

6. When feeling this emotion again, reflect on what you are telling yourself. If it is negative, how could you reframe your self-talk to be more positive?

Practice your positive self-talk frequently in your mind, or even in the mirror. This reinforces the positive, and in time means you will automatically think positively, rather than negatively when that situation recurs.

Don't beat yourself up when you react to a negative emotion. It is what it is, and with the best will in the world, we all succumb at times. Be realistic: understand it and learn from it.

Activity: Your reflections

It is time again to reflect on your thoughts and the activities you have completed in this section.

Review them in the light of the following questions and record your answers below:

- What have you learned about yourself in this chapter?
- What do you need to change?
- What do you need to start doing that you have not done before?
- What other thoughts do you have?

Part

2

What I think

6: Self-care

Do you:

- Find work demands are overwhelming you right now?
- Wake in the night because you have so much on your mind?
- Push back on socialising with family and friends because you have too much to do?
- Need coffee, strong tea or some alcohol to keep you going?
- Feel utterly exhausted but struggle on?
- Find your mind isn't working as well as it could – maybe you're forgetting things or you're finding it hard to concentrate?

If the answer to any of these is Yes, then you need to pay special attention to this chapter.

There is so much going on in a Young Professional's highly aspirational career that it's very easy to forget to take care of yourself along the way.

There has been a lot of research over the years that tells us that engagement and wellbeing are inextricably linked to performance. If you over-engage by throwing yourself into your work every waking hour, with little time for relaxation and recovery, your mental and physical capacities will eventually become depleted.

This is burnout. When you burn out, you no longer have the capacity to cope or withstand the pressure.

If you healthily engage with work in a way that uses your skills and talents to the utmost, whilst also caring for, and managing your physical and mental wellbeing, then you will have lots of energy and be at your most productive.

Self-care is the physical and mental aspect of wellbeing. Without self-care, your wellbeing is compromised and you cannot hope to perform at your best.

How we think affects how we cope under stress

If you are not performing at your best, you will damage your career. To stand any hope of managing the demands of a high performing career, you have got to know what you're thinking.

This thinking is two-fold; firstly, maintaining a healthy attitude towards the highly demanding, chaotic world of work and secondly, making time regularly to reflect on how you feel physically and mentally.

Self-care requires you to manage the way you respond to stressful events in your life. This requires you to have strong, flexible attitudes to the situation or person causing you discomfort. An attitude is a pretty settled way of thinking, based on the evaluation you make of your experiences, beliefs, feelings and values. Your attitude is your version of a situation which shapes the way you subsequently behave.

What's going on in your head?

Attitudes are completely individual and can only be formed by ourselves. They are hidden away in our subconscious minds where we basically let them get on with it, working away automatically below the surface. It is only when faced with a new event or situation, or something that is not as it should be, that we switch to conscious mode and give any thought to our attitudes.

Attitudes are a mindset that can be positive or negative. They can empower you or limit you; because what you think and tell yourself, you will do. They tell you what you can, can't, ought and ought not to do and as a result, you can end up jumping to conclusions, blowing things out of proportion, labelling yourself unfairly or unjustly blaming yourself for something - all of which unnecessarily stresses you.

Therefore, by understanding how you think, you can enhance your resilience and wellbeing.

Case study

Yasmine was a 26 year old accountant who had been thrilled when she got her job with a high profile city firm on graduation. The job was tough, though. It involved long hours and juggling lots of clients who expected a response to their email at any time of the day or night and because everyone was so busy, her manager would often appear, asking her to do something extra for a client to which she felt she couldn't say no.

To compound the pressure, she was in a highly competitive environment. To stand any chance of promotion soon, she needed to demonstrate just how good she was. This meant everything she did had to be perfect, so she spent extra time checking her work for mistakes and making sure what she did put her in the best possible light. These demands made it hard to leave the office at a reasonable time. In fact, she was no longer sure what was a reasonable time, because everyone worked late.

Her friends had stopped asking her to join them for a night out because she always said no. She hadn't had a proper holiday, with a complete break from work, since she'd started working for the firm. As a result, she was exhausted.

Then, on top of everything, her boyfriend emailed her to say that she was now boring to be with and if she didn't change, he wasn't sure that he could be with her any longer.

Part

2

What I think

What was happening here?

Yasmine was suffering from stress and more than likely on the road to burnout. Stress had blocked her logical thinking and she was losing touch with reality. Much of this came from the demands of a professional job, but a lot came from her own misconceptions of how she had to perform to get noticed and promoted. Saying no, avoiding perfectionism and managing your time effectively are three powerful ways to manage pressure when you're an aspiring Young Professional.

Top tips for self-care

- Maintaining a positive attitude is at the heart of resilience. It isn't challenging situations and difficult people in themselves that cause stress. It's how you personally interpret the situation in your head.
- Learn to understand how you respond to pressure and to notice the effects it is having on you mentally and physically.
- Deal with the chaos and manage your workload by prioritising key tasks and deliverables, and controlling digital technology.
- Keep physically healthy. This means eating healthy, blood sugar balancing foods, getting plenty of sleep and taking regular exercise.
- If you are finding it hard to identify the underlying causes of your stress, keep a stress diary. Make a record of the triggers and your response to them. Review at the end of each day and tell yourself how you will respond more positively in the future.
- Keep in contact with people. Ask questions, share problems, make sure you socialise with family and friends. To ensure survival, humans are social creatures. Check that you are not pulling back from people and isolating yourself.

Activity: Stress and me

1. On a scale of 1-10 where 1 is not at all and 10 is extremely, how stressed are you feeling right now?

Not at all									Extremely
1	2	3	4	5	6	7	8	9	10

2. How would you know you are stressed? What signs and symptoms do you display? To help with this, think about how you physically respond, then about how you think and feel and respond socially.

3. How do you manage stress?

When dealing with stressful situations, you need to dig deep and unpick why you are responding in the way you are. That means understanding why you have interpreted the situation in the way you have. What's really going on in your head?

4. What triggers stress in you? Think about people, situations, worries you have and the aspects of a situation that you find difficult.

5. Why do you react the way you do?

6. Capture your thoughts.

Part

2

What I think

Activity: Your personal perspective on stress

Stress stems from our personal attitudes. Because our attitudes are very specific to us, we will each respond to the same situation differently. However, from my experience, there are some themes we can look at that enable us to categorise our stress type.

1. Have a look at the four Personality and Stress Types on the following pages. You will identify which one type most closely describes you. No one type outshines another or is preferable to another; each one has its plus points and its challenges.

2. When you have chosen the type that best describes you, record at the bottom of the chart how you show the characteristics of this type. Add examples of when you have reacted in these ways.

Personality: RESULTS-DRIVEN   Stress Type: OVER-ASSERTIVE

Personality:
- Tough minded, dominating, independent
- Focused and determined
- High energy and attitude
- Know what they want and go out to get it
- Competitive and high achievers; love work
- Like to take charge and be in control of the job and of people
- Goal-focused rather than people -focused
- Good decision makers

Stressors:
- Micro-management
- Incompetence – manager and line reports
- Not delivering on a promise
- Over-emotional responses in others
- Slow pace
- Criticism
- Poorly defined criteria
- Disorganisation
- Lack of recognition for effort and achievements

Symptoms:
- Shows anger
- Becomes domineering
- Becomes inflexible
- Isolates
- Starts to obsess over detail
- Churns previous events over in their head
- Sudden emotional or aggressive outbursts: usually involving 'poor me'

Why you are this type:

Part

2

What I think

Personality: FACTS-DRIVEN   **Stress Type: OVER-ANALYTICAL**

Personality:
- Focused on thinking and analysis
- All about detail and facts with a good memory for these
- Logical, organised and orderly: likes to be in charge of own schedule
- Task-focused not people-focused
- Values efficiency and consistency
- Prefers routine and tried and tested ways of doing things than the unknown
- Can be critical and detached, or reserved
- Likes a quiet workplace with few interruptions to thinking processes
- Can become obsessive about task in hand
- Suspicious of the future and of creativity

Stressors:
- Unsubstantiated ideas where you have to imagine the outcome
- Winging it with no chance to prepare
- Over-committing so not enough time to give to each item
- Early deadlines without time to provide the detail and do the work justice
- Having to predict the future without evidence
- Unclear direction and instructions
- Lack of accuracy/attention to detail in others' work
- Brainstorming
- Expecting that sense should be made of others' wacky ideas

Symptoms:
- Overdoes the detail and cannot let go - ending up paralysed
- Negative and pessimistic about straightforward matters
- Blames and accuses others
- Anxious with sense of impending doom and disaster
- Fails to listen and misinterprets what others are saying (mind so focused on own thoughts)
- Becomes withdrawn and isolated from others
- Reads meaning into things that are not there
- Loses sleep due to worrying
- Depression
- Eventually becomes inaccurate and unreliable as burnout approaches

Why you are this type:

Part

2

What I think

Personality: RELATIONSHIP-DRIVEN   **Stress Type: OVER-SENSITIVE**

Personality:
- Sociable, approachable, warm
- Dependable and supportive
- Will give, give, give but likes to be appreciated and valued
- Likes harmony and to keep the peace
- Will avoid confrontation and uncomfortable conversations
- Aware of how actions can affect others, reads people well
- Likes to help others whenever possible
- Can express own emotions openly and is comfortable when others do so
- Has strong personal values and convictions and will stick by these
- Likes to feel involved

Stressors:
- A bad atmosphere or conflict
- Controlling, confrontational, critical people
- Highly political environment with 'watch your back' undercurrents
- Unjustified criticism or being undermined or belittled by someone
- Being kept out of the loop
- Being expected to compromise values or personal convictions
- Change – particularly if affecting people
- Too much emphasis on productivity or the bottom line rather than people
- Time pressures that make it difficult to do the job that would please people or match their own expectations of a job well done

Symptoms:
- Compulsive search for answers to why things are this way
- Loss of confidence, so competence suffers
- Becomes more anxious, then judgemental, critical or cynical about self first then about others as stress continues
- Starts to become more cynical and finds fault (eg reasons why an idea won't work and should not be supported)
- Acts/talks without concern for how others will feel
- Depression and feelings of helplessness

Why you are this type:

Personality: ATTENTION-DRIVEN   Stress Type: OVER-INDULGENT

Personality:
- Enthusiastic, stimulating, exciting, personable
- Self aware and people aware
- Has a vision with good instinct/gut feeling
- Looks to the future with optimism
- Imaginative and creative
- Prefers a flexible approach to work with control over how the work is to be carried out
- Works well with people but prefers autonomy unless someone is fully in tune with their thinking
- Loves variety and change – hates routine and having to follow delivery through to the end
- Will make their ideas and feelings known

Stressors:
- Having to work with too much detail
- Being expected to follow-through with routine work
- Finding themselves overcommitted so unable to be creative
- Unpredictable demands on their time
- Being micro-managed
- Being mistrusted or having their competence doubted
- Obstinate, irrational people
- Strict rules with prescribed ways of doing the work
- Unchallenging work

Symptoms:

- Feel out of control and overwhelmed
- Starts to anticipate the worst to the extent that things are seen as impossible
- Generally unable to identify the source of the problem
- Begin to internalise physical symptoms (headaches, tummy problems) until they eventually feel they are life- threatening
- Becomes obsessive and over-indulges in food/alcohol/exercise, causing harm to the body
- Sees the world and everyone in it as their enemy
- Insomnia: unable to switch off from problems
- Muscular tension
- Depression, then eventually withdrawal and burnout

Why you are this type:

Part

2

What I think

3. Find your Personality and Stress Type below and practice the tips.

As well as helping you to cope with stress better, you could also use these charts to understand other people's behaviour when under stress. This then improves the way you work with them. For example, if a colleague is a Results-Driven type, make sure you always deliver when you promised to.

Personality: RESULTS-DRIVEN   **Solution: WORK WITH OTHERS**
Symptoms: OVER ASSERTIVE

- Think logically and prioritise what's important to you and the task.
- Talk to someone and get an independent perspective to clear your head.
- Allow others to contribute and help you – don't keep trying to do everything alone.
- Learn to listen. Others can help and could have constructive ideas
- Learn to coach others to develop their strengths – this is an investment in your future.
- Become more interdependent and less independent.
- Stop and take stock of the feelings of others. If you can develop empathy and rapport, colleagues will work with you rather than against you.

Personality: FACTS-DRIVEN   **Solution: MOVE TO ACTION**
Symptoms: OVER ANALYTICAL

- Stop and take stock. What is real and what is imagined?
- Stop working to such depth of detail – draw a line, make a decision and move to action.
- Set a deadline to move to action regardless of the state of play.
- Consciously get away from it all: go for a pleasurable walk, do some gardening, listen to some music.
- Prioritise and allow others to determine what is important.
- Delegate more of the detail.
- Share your thoughts with a trusted other – ask for help or explore possibilities with them.
- Use your logic rather than detail and evidence.

Personality: RELATIONSHIPS-DRIVEN **Solution: REFOCUS ON**
Symptoms: OVER SENSITIVE **THE POSITIVE**

- Stop and take stock. Are you being over sensitive?
- Refocus on what's going right – not what's going wrong.
- Consider the impact of your behaviour on others – are you comfortable with this?
- Try to hide how upset you are – you can't always wear your heart on your sleeve.
- Confide in a friend or trusted other who can tell you what's really happening.
- Take yourself away from it – go for a walk, meditate or do yoga.
- Record your feelings in a journal and reflect on what this means and the impact on yourself and others.
- Build a relationship with your line manager so you can elicit honest feedback. Take this as feedback and not criticism.
- Ask for help – you offer it to others, you are also entitled to it.

Personality: ATTENTION-DRIVEN **Solution: LIGHTEN UP**
Symptoms: OVER INDULGENT

- Use your creativity to find a different approach. Always look for the opportunity to grow – this will reignite your motivation.
- Lighten up – if you're taking things too seriously, you're on your way down. Think logically to get your perspective back.
- Allow others to help you with the detail.
- Prioritise what you need to do and delegate the follow-through.
- Make lists/use workflow systems so that you can see what needs to be done, rather than having it all in your head.
- Create some space – take some time out to rest, meditate, improve your diet, take light exercise.
- Get some coaching as a sounding board to reality.
- Encourage feedback.

Part

2

What I think

Activity: Your 'urgents' and 'importants'

Do you find that there are not enough hours in the day to get everything done?

Are you getting to work early, staying late and constantly firing up your computer at home just to keep on top of everything?

If so, that's a perfect recipe for burnout. Working this way is not necessarily because you have too much to do. It may well be because you are failing to organise your time and prioritise your activities sufficiently well.

To do this, you need to identify your tasks according to the following categories:

a. **Important and urgent.** These are the tasks that have to be done now. If you find yourself always working on urgent and important tasks, then you are likely to find yourself overwhelmed, constantly under pressure and fire-fighting because so many activities demand your immediate attention. These activities leave you exhausted and without any sense of accomplishment. It is exceptionally hard to create a resilient career when you spend too much of your time here.

b. **Important but not urgent.** These are the tasks you plan for, then deliver in a well-paced way so that you do not experience any last minute madness. Working this way allows you time to think creatively. Part of this time for creativity will be space to reflect and plan your career. This is where resilient careers are made.

c. **Urgent but not important.** This is someone else's urgent task that they are asking you to do. If you're working on tasks here, it's because you haven't said a polite no! Always saying 'yes' will send you straight into 'urgent and important', stress you out and leave you feeling very cross with yourself for agreeing. Remember, if it is not part of your remit, then that person will get the credit for this work, not you. If you want a truly resilient career, you need to know when to say no and make sure you say it.

d. **Not important and not urgent.** These are the trivial tasks which do nothing for your career value. You might end up working on these because you're bored with your job. Maybe you're not using your strengths to the full, or maybe procrastinating so that you fail to accomplish anything. There's every chance this is because you cannot sustain working at an urgent and important pace relentlessly, so you've come here for a rest. To get yourself away from here, you need to create tasks that use your strengths and grow your interest, without which your career will stagnate.

Getting your priorities right

Look at your current to-do list. Include the tasks to complete within your role, meetings, emails, answering queries and anything else that is within your remit.

Assign each task to the relevant quadrant.

Important but not urgent	Important and urgent
Not important but urgent	**Not important and not urgent**

Now you have a snapshot of your priorities - what do you see?

Do all the activities relate to your job goals?

Do you have important tasks that need doing but you are procrastinating over? If so, you need to prioritise and allocate time to accomplish these.

Do the important tasks when you first come into the office in the morning. Prioritise these important tasks over checking and answering emails; emails can be done when you need to take a break from concentrated effort.

Remember, you are judged on what you deliver, not on the time you spend wading through emails.

1. **Prioritise your tasks.** What is the most important to accomplish? Determine this by knowing what your goals are, then prioritise tasks according to these.

    Score the most urgent and important a number one, then the next a number two and so on. Do not procrastinate and distract yourself with meaningless tasks - get on and get these done. It will make you feel good to have accomplished them, and this will energise you.

2. **What can you clear from your to-do list?** Do you need to have a conversation with your manager about this? Could you organise your time better? What could you delegate? What could you pass back to the real owner?

3. **Keep a diary or record.** Whatever you are asked to do should be itemised in your diary.

    This includes all big tasks, deadlines and appointments. It is important for your wellbeing that you make this diary a life diary, so include non-work obligations and appointments and stick to them. Otherwise, they will very easily become sidelined. Look at your diary and say no to requests for help if you do not have the capacity to fulfil them.

If that is difficult, negotiate something that will work for both of you. Always make sure that what you schedule in your diary are:

- the activities that will take you towards achieving your goals
- the activities that will help you recharge and recover.

4. **Record how you use your time.** Do not forget to include how long you spend on emails, at meetings, on digital technology and on the phone, as well as sorting problems and enquiries. Having an overview will help you see when things are unbalanced and too much time is being spent on non-productive activities.

Part

2

What I think

Activity: Your reflections

It is time again to reflect on your thoughts and the activities you have completed in this chapter.

Review the chapter in light of the following questions and record your answers below:

- What have you learned about yourself in this chapter?
- What do you need to change?
- What do you need to start doing that you have not done before?
- What other thoughts do you have?

Part

2

What I think

Part 3
What I do

7: My career capital

You've spent a lot of time considering who you are, the values you hold, and what you think. That's powerful and important groundwork. It's in the doing that you grow in capability, confidence and reputation, enhancing your career and making you more successful and satisfied with how it is progressing.

'Doing' is where you build your energy and resilience. As a Young Professional, by taking responsibility for the 'doing,' you become your own unique person. Your sense of purpose and meaning grow, the framework of your career develops and your identity as a professional emerges. All this builds your resilience so you can cope with whatever the world of work may throw at you.

- Do you want a promotion but you never know what to highlight on the application form?
- Do you do your job without thinking about the value you give to your employer?
- Do you feel that you don't get a chance to use your strengths?
- Do you think that the best way to grow your career is to move job frequently?
- Are you bored with your work or career?

113

If the answer to any of these is Yes, then you need to pay special attention to this chapter.

As a Young Professional it is not your job title, job role or even your profession that defines you, but your career capital.

Career capital is like a bank account. Rather than containing money, the value comes from the collection of personal qualities, skills, knowledge, training, experiences, achievements and relationships that you have to offer your employer and the broader marketplace. It's the nature of career capital that determines your financial worth.

Career capital is something that develops over the course of your career. With every new assignment you work on, every new skill you develop, every new bit of learning that takes place, you build your career capital further. It is what makes you unique and distinctive. So long as you are also robust, it makes you unbelievably valuable. I think of it as the very definition of your success.

This section helps you assess the career capital you currently hold, and think about ways to grow and develop it.

Career capital gives you confidence

Growing your career is not about frequently changing job, although if the timing is right and this is a good move then this can certainly help. It's about building up the knowledge, skills and relationships in your career capital account.

This requires continuous effort, planning and reflection to capture what you have and what you need. Ignore this, and your career stagnates. This means your account plummets in value.

Develop it and you enhance your marketability and can do anything you want to do. That's because career capital equates to confidence. You have it, it's of value and you can use it. It creates authenticity which helps you with choices and decision-making.

High value career capital is a must-have if you want a truly outstanding and resilient career.

Case study

Dev knew there was an opportunity coming up in another department and was very interested in it. One day, whilst walking to the lift, he came face to face with the manager of one of the teams in that department. The manager said that he liked what Dev had to say in the meeting last week and thought he should consider applying for the job vacancy.

Dev felt embarrassed so he tried to brush the compliment off by saying that it wasn't his idea. It had been a team effort and he'd played an insignificant part. The manager walked away bemused. Dev gave more thought to applying for the job, but eventually concluded that it would be a waste of time as everyone else had so much more to offer.

What was happening here?

Dev was not aware of the value he had to offer this organisation. When he was complimented, he brushed it off as someone else's capital.

We all have a value created by our competences, knowledge and experience. By knowing what this is through defining our career capital, we have the collateral on hand to complete the application for a great new job.

Top tips for developing your career capital

- Review your career capital account regularly – just as you would with your bank account (hopefully).

- Pay into your career capital account regularly. This means adding new knowledge on a monthly basis; a skill or relationship that enhances you. It does not have to be something mega, such as gaining a new qualification, just a steady stream of small chunks of value.

- If funds have not grown for a while, or are getting low because you are falling behind others, then you are not growing your career; you're stagnating. Whatever you do, if you want a resilient career as a Young Professional, don't allow this to happen.

Part
3

What I do

You could:
- take on new tasks
- gain some knowledge by reading a business book
- get yourself on an in-house training course
- complete a course on the training platform
- join a project where you could learn from others.

How much are you worth (in career capital terms)?

Activity: How competent are you?

Competency is your ability to undertake or do something successfully. Competencies come from your talents and skills.

A talent is a natural ability to do something without too much thought. A skill is a learned proficiency or ability that is acquired or developed through training or experience.

An example might be a international footballer, who will undoubtedly have started out with a great natural talent for playing football. Not everyone has this, and it's a big advantage, but to become a true star, the footballer then developed a variety of skills through coaching and practice.

Your talents and skills

Use the chart on the following page to identify which words define a talent or skill you have. Don't be distracted by everything in the list that you can do. This is about identifying areas where you truly stand out.

In the T/S column, mark T if it is a talent you naturally have, or S if it is a skill you acquired.

	T/S			T/S
Accurate		Delegating		
Action planning		Demonstrating		
Adaptable		Dependable		
Administrating		Designing		
Advising		Determining		
Agile		Documenting		
Analysis		Driving		
Articulating		Editing		
Assembling		Efficient		
Assertive		Empathising		
Aware		Empowering		
Brainstorming ideas		Energising		
Budgeting		Estimating		
Chairing		Ethical		
Checking		Explaining		
Clear thinking		Evaluating		
Clear speech		Filing		
Coaching		Financially astute		
Collaborating		Flexible		
Collating		Forecasting		
Commercially aware		Foreign language skills		
Communicating non-verbally		Friendly		
Communicating verbally		Global skills		
Computing		Goal setting		
Confident		Helpful		
Concise		Honest		
Constructing		Humorous		
Controlling		Implementing		
Coping		Improving		
Counselling		Independent		
Creative		Information technology		
Data handling		Initiating		
Decision-making				

Part
3

What I do

	T/S		T/S
Innovating		Providing feedback	
Installing		Public speaking	
Interpersonal skills		Punctual	
Interpreting		Questioning	
Investigating		Reconciling	
Judging		Reflecting	
Lateral thinking		Relating	
Leading		Reliability	
Learning quickly		Report writing	
Listening		Researching	
Logical thinking		Resilient	
Managing people		Resolving conflict	
Managing conflict		Resourceful	
Managing time		Respectful	
Marketing		Responsible	
Mediating		Risk assessment	
Mentoring		Selling	
Motivating		Scheduling	
Negotiating		Self-aware	
Networking		Self-controlling	
Numerical		Self-disciplining	
Open-minded		Self-motivating	
Organising		Summarising	
Patient		Teamworking	
Persuading		Technical	
Persisting		Telephoning	
Piloting		Thinking ahead	
Planning		Training	
Positive		Trusting others	
Prioritising		Versatile	
Problem-solving		Visualising	
Promoting		Working to deadlines	
		Working under pressure	
		Written communication	

Pick out your talents and list them.

Write down the value you bring to your employer when using these talents. Think of specific examples to demonstrate this.

Put a star by the talents you consider are a real strength and distinguish you from anyone else. These are your areas of peak performance, which will energise you.

Then pick out your skills and list them.

Write down the value you bring to your employer when using these skills. Think of specific examples to demonstrate this.

Put a star by the skills you consider are a real strength and distinguish you from anyone else. These are the things you perform well at and which give both energy and confidence.

Aim to cultivate - and always have on tap, ready to use - two to three talents and skills that you excel at. You can use these at the drop of a hat to help yourself, your team or the organisation out of a difficult situation. This is what gets you noticed and highlights your potential.

Part

3

What I do

Activity: Your work qualities

Look at these words and highlight the ones that describe you. Each of these words is a personal quality and all have value so there are no right or wrong answers. Add anything that is missing that you think is an important description of you.

Adaptable	Independent
Analytical	Interpersonally able
Attentive to detail	Has leadership skills
Calm	Good listener
Cautious	Loyal
Cheerful	Management skills
Committed	Well-mannered
Cooperative	Demonstrates maturity
Creative	Open
Detail-orientated	Participative
Determined	Good planning skills
Diligent	Positive attitude
Diversity-sensitive	Problem solving skills
Driven	Professional
Effective communicator	Punctual
Empathetic	Reflective
Energetic	Resilient
Enthusiastic	Respectful
Financially responsible	Supportive
Flexible	Teamworker
Follows through	Tenacious
Goes the extra mile	Thoughtful
Good judgement	Truthful
Happy	Trustworthy
Humorous	Versatile
Imaginative	Well-organised

What value are your qualities to an employer?

Think about examples when you have used these qualities. What advantages did they bring?

The aim of this exercise is to identify who you are. By reading the descriptions you can also begin to understand the qualities others have. They may be different to yours but by knowing this, you are more likely to be more accepting of them.

Just because others are different does not make them inferior or wrong. Difference is what makes up life's rich tapestry.

Activity: Your training and qualifications

What training have you undertaken? Think about everything: professional and non-professional, qualification-based and non-qualification-based.

1. What non-training development have you received? This could include coaching from your manager or possibly learning by working alongside a colleague.

Training	Value it brings
Development	**Value it brings**

What specific value **do you** bring to an employer by having these? How are you currently using them?

Activity: Your knowledge

1. What are the ways you learn – tick all that apply

   - By studying for qualifications
   - By attending training courses
   - By e-learning courses on a training platform
   - By reading
   - By listening to broadcasts/books
   - From experience, by doing something
   - By watching what others do, then copying them
   - By engaging with a coach or mentor

2. What do you know that adds value but might not be common knowledge? This could include both fact and rumours! Knowledge is power. Picking up workplace rumours can mean you have your ear to the ground, but be careful to distinguish the reality.

3. How much you know is important to your capacity to deliver your role successfully. Your knowledge can include technical, product, services and customer information, facts about your team including your manager, about the organisation, your industry or sector that might not be common knowledge.

Whenever I run management and leadership programmes, the first thing I ask participants at the beginning of the first workshop, and before I introduce myself, is what has anyone found out about me. We need to know more than just what's going on in front of our noses!

Part

3

What I do

Activity: Your relationship skills

You cannot work in a vacuum, so relationship skills are a great asset to your career capital account. What skills do you use when interacting with people? Think about communication, engagement, influencing, managing and trust building skills.

Activity: Your external experience

What experience do you have outside your work environment that can add to your career capital? This may be gained from a number of activities such as voluntary work, running a sports team or overseas travel.

Activity: Your contacts

Who are your useful contacts, internally and externally to the organisation, on whom you could call on if required?

What I do

Activity: Your achievements

What have you done that has meant you have made a successful contribution to your employer?

These successes are your achievements. They are of high value in your career capital account. The things you have been responsible for, the risks you've taken and seen pay off, the positive feedback you've received and the awards, commendations or special mentions you've received get you noticed.

Only you will see what you write down here. So go for it - it's time to blow your own trumpet!

Successful outcomes from my responsibilities:

Successful outcomes from taking a risk:

Successful outcome from meeting challenges:

Recognition/feedback I've received:

Awards, commendations and special mentions:

Highlight the five achievements that mean the most to you.

Why are you particularly proud of each of these achievements?

What did you do to get the outcome you did?

If this flags up some new talents, skills and abilities, then add them where appropriate to previous exercises.

Part

3

What I do

Activity: The value you bring to your employer

What value do you personally add to the company you currently work for? Think about what makes you unique and special.

Activity: Your reflections

It is time again to reflect on your thoughts and the activities you have completed in this chapter.

Review the chapter in light of the following questions and record your answers below:

- What have you learned about yourself in this chapter?
- What value do you hold in your career capital account?
- What is missing from your account?
- What do you need to do to raise the value of your career capital account?
- What do you need to change?
- What other thoughts do you have?

Part

3

What I do

8: My reputation

- Do you stammer when someone unexpectedly asks you to say a bit about yourself?
- Do you prefer to keep your head down and get on with your tasks?
- Do you prefer not to openly talk about your achievements in case people think you're bragging?
- Do you find it difficult to understand why people need to be emotional?
- Do you frequently find yourself embroiled in conflict?
- Do you avoid 'office politics'?

If the answer to any of these is Yes, then you need to pay special attention to this chapter.

Your reputation is the degree of esteem in which you are held by those to whom you are connected. It is one of the most important elements of a resilient career and absolutely essential if you want your career to be outstanding.

You cannot hope to progress your career without the support and recognition of others. The higher the regard in which you are held, the better. This is your value in a competitive marketplace.

You may want your name to be the one anyone in authority thinks of first – that's the highest order of esteem – but you cannot sit back and wait for it. Nor will it 'just happen' because you think you are doing a good job. You have to work for it. It's the effort you put in that will distinguish you from other high achievers with potential.

Case Study

Sam was a capable sales executive who hit his targets regularly and was pretty good with his customers too. He'd noticed that there was a small group of people, which included his own manager, who regularly left their desks and went into a huddle in another room. Sam had never been invited to join them and as time went on, despite knowing he was well regarded, he felt more and more of an outsider.

One day, Sam was experiencing some challenges closing one of his sales deals. He'd been working on it for months and it was so close. His manager offered to make a call and hey presto, the deal was done. The manager told Sam that as he had closed the deal, he would be taking the credit for it. This meant the manager would earn the commission.

Late that afternoon he saw the group gathering and walking towards the room to go into their huddle and as they met they patted the manager on the back and laughed. At that point, Sam felt that his only option was to change job.

What was happening here?

Sam was experiencing company politics and the meeting of the inner circle. Rather than thinking that the only way to cope was to find a new job, Sam should have found ways to ingratiate himself to these people by asking questions, showing an interest in what they were working on and showing the value he brought to the company. To make him feel better about their huddles, he could have reframed the situation as a group meeting to support each other.

Top tips for building your reputation

You cannot succeed in this competitive world unless you put yourself forward. Hiding away in your office will not do you any favours. You create the image you want people to see when they look at you. People are not mind readers, so having the right image will count for nothing unless you let people know about your career intentions and what you want to achieve. Fail to do so, and they'll be drawn to the person who has made this clear.

1. Build positive relationships using good communication skills, so that you are respected, trusted and listened to.
2. Deal with conflict along the way. It throws a painful hit at your reputation if you let things fester or dogmatically stick to your opinion.
3. Be aware of the internal political culture of your workplace. It's a shark pool out there as everyone vies for the position that will give them the greatest reward.

Your image

Your image is the brand you create around what you have to offer. It sums up what makes you distinctive, and it's incredibly valuable.

Companies are becoming adept at creating a brand around their company name or the products they offer. There's usually a smart, catchy statement that makes them distinguishable. If it's done well, it's extremely powerful. This is what we need to do for ourselves.

For a Young Professional, a strong brand identity is a 'must have'. A personal brand statement provides you with the collateral to market yourself confidently whenever you're put on the spot by being asked for information about yourself and your career. With a little forethought, who you are, the value you add and your goals can be expressed in a compact statement, providing you with the opportunity to intrigue and impress the person you're in communication with.

Activity: Defining your personal brand

1. This is your opportunity to write your brand statement. Create a short but vibrant statement using a sentence to cover each of the following points. Think about the career capital exercises you completed earlier. What is unique and valuable in your career capital that you can leverage?

   a. What do you do?
   b. What are you good at?
   c. How do you add value to your employer?
   d. What makes you distinctive?
   e. What are your career aspirations?

2. Once your brand statement is clear, record it where you will see it often. A good place is your screensaver on the devices you regularly use. You could also use paper or card, coloured pens, highlighters - whatever you would like that makes it stand out in a special way. Then put it where you'll see it often: inside your wardrobe door, on the fridge, in your desk.

3. Whenever you see it, rehearse it. It needs to be on the tip of your tongue at all times.

4. Use something from it as a positive intention to start each day. This will energise you and focus your mind on career success.

Positive relationships

"People will forget what you said, people will forget what you did. But people will never forget how you made them feel."
Maya Angelou

When building your reputation, you need to be aware of the role relationships can play. Everyone you come into contact with plays a part. You cannot work in cooperation with some and be off-hand with others.

Good working relationships are crucial for career resilience. How you get on with people will determine how you are perceived and how influential you can be. Do this well and it will enhance your reputation. Do it badly and no matter what you do to show you do a good job, you'll have no influence.

Generating strong relationships is far from easy. People are complex and idiosyncratic. Each of us has our own expectations and ways of doing things and can change opinions with the wind. You cannot expect people to treat you in the way you would like to be treated.

You need to take control of each relationship yourself. By communicating well, listening attentively, showing empathy and dealing proactively with conflict, you will soon become adept at interacting with others.

Activity: Relationship Skills

Think of someone at work who you think has particularly good relationship skills. Look at the questions below and record your answers in the chart.

1. What characteristics does this person exhibit?
2. How do you compare to this person?
3. What can you learn from them? What do you need to do differently?

Person	Characteristics	How do you compare?	What do you need to do?

Activity: Relationships

We are going to examine your starting point: where you are now, with the people around you at work? Be as honest as you can. We will look at any improvements that are needed, and how to achieve them.

1. Think about the relationships that are most important for enhancing your career. Record the names of these key people in the box below.
2. What do you think about them? What is the state of the relationship? How do you behave when interacting with them? Be as honest as you can.

Name	The state of the relationship

Good relating starts with empathy. Empathy means that you identify with and understand the other person's situation, feelings and motives by putting yourself in their shoes.

Empathy begins with attentively tuning in to the person you are interacting with and use the information you glean from them to act with consideration towards them. It requires active listening. This means you not only listen to the words they say, but show genuine interest in understanding what the other person thinks, feels or wants.

Empathy is a powerful route to creating positive relationships. If you want to grow your reputation and influence, you need to think beyond yourself, manage your emotions (which we covered in Chapter 5), understand the other person's perspective by listening and asking questions, and respond in a way that achieves a win-win outcome.

Part

3

What I do

Activity: How empathetic are you?

Complete the following questionnaire about your empathy skills. Circle the number that reflects the degree to which you agree with each statement using:

1 = Strongly disagree
2 = Disagree
3 = Neutral
4 = Agree
5 = Strongly agree

Is this you?					
1. I am interested in knowing more about other people.	1	2	3	4	5
2. I try to understand how people think and feel.	1	2	3	4	5
3. I try to see things from the other person's point of view.	1	2	3	4	5
4. I listen and try to understand what people have to say.	1	2	3	4	5
5. I show sympathy when someone is sad or upset	1	2	3	4	5
6. I consider the other person's feelings before saying or doing something.	1	2	3	4	5
7. I try to make people feel at ease when interacting with me.	1	2	3	4	5
8. I try to understand how and why people think and behave differently to me.	1	2	3	4	5

9.	I always give my full attention to someone when they are talking to me.	1	2	3	4	5
10.	I am sensitive to why something has upset someone.	1	2	3	4	5
11.	Before saying or doing something, I consider how others may feel as a result.	1	2	3	4	5
12.	I allow people to tell me their point of view.	1	2	3	4	5
13.	I show I appreciate the other person's view, even if I don't agree with it.	1	2	3	4	5
14.	I remain calm and listen when someone is angry.	1	2	3	4	5
15.	If there's conflict, I like to hear other people's opinions.	1	2	3	4	5
16.	I can tell if someone wants to say something and I give them the opportunity to talk.	1	2	3	4	5
17.	I am sensitive to how people are reacting when I am making my point.	1	2	3	4	5
18.	I am aware when someone's mood is changing.	1	2	3	4	5
19.	I consider the impact my decisions may have on other people.	1	2	3	4	5
20.	I control my moods and feelings.	1	2	3	4	5
	TOTAL					

Part
3

What I do

Add up your scores to get an overall final score.

80-100 indicates that you have well-developed empathy skills.

60-79 indicates that your empathy skills could be improved. If you want to build strong, influential relationships, look at the areas in which you scored 3 or less. Consider how you could begin to practice these behaviours.

20-59 indicates that empathy is not one of your skills. Consider signing up for an emotional intelligence course to learn more about this subject. You could also ask for some feedback from people you know and trust on how you are perceived and what needs to change. Begin by practicing just one of the skills most commonly suggested, such as listening or showing consideration.

If you find the concept of empathy difficult, keep a diary, and each day make a record of an interaction that took place. Consider the following:

- What was the situation?
- How did I behave?
- What questions did I ask?
- What does that person think, feel, want?
- How did the interaction end?

Managing conflict

We are all different, and it just isn't realistic to expect everyone to live as you do. Others do not have the same desires and expectations as you.

Conflict takes place when opinions, perspectives and expectations contradict, resulting in disagreement or dispute. If you are going to build positive relationships, you need to manage conflict.

It may be possible to prevent conflict occurring in the first place, by behaviours such as not taking what someone has said personally, but there are times when conflict does occur.

At such times, find ways to take the heat out of the situation and create an environment where all parties can come to agreement on how to move forward. In other words, use the empathy skills we discussed earlier in this chapter.

It is often the case that angry people calm down when they find they are being listened to. And when all else fails, it may be that you have to say: 'Let's agree to disagree agreeably'.

Activity: Your behaviour

Think about someone you find yourself in conflict with. What impact is this having on the relationship?

1. Think about yourself

   • Why does this happen, and what is going on?
   • What part are you playing in the situation – what are you saying and doing that may incite conflict?
   • How does it make you feel?
   • What is likely to happen if you don't deal with this now?

2. Now put yourself in the other person's shoes

   • What part are you playing?
   • When they look at the situation, what are they seeing?
   • How are they feeling?

3. Now position yourself as an observer looking across the room at both of you

   • What do you see taking place between these two people?
   • What could be done to resolve the matter?

Part
3

What I do

4. What will you do?

It helps to prepare for difficult conversations in advance and practice what you want to say in the mirror to build your confidence. When you meet the other party, acknowledge their point of view first, before you share yours, then look to how you can solve the situation and move on. Be aware that you cannot change people, only yourself, so be brave and seek to be part of the solution and not the problem. Others will notice and respect you for this.

Conflict resolution is not about being too 'nice' or always being the one to capitulate. Certain people will exploit this. It's about being both assertive, so you still get your point across, but also solution-focused, to reach agreement between all sides.

Activity: Dealing with a toxic boss

As a Young Professional, working for a negative, unhelpful or bullying boss can be a miserable and lonely place.

1. Look at the list below. What behaviours do you recognise in your boss? (This could be your direct line manager, or someone more senior you may be working with or regularly come into contact with) Do they...?

- Focus on themselves – it's all about them.
- Have a win/lose mentality – have to be seen to be a winner at all costs.
- Plays games with people – such as criticising employees in front of others.
- Abuse their position – behave well when dealing with powerful people and badly when dealing with less powerful people.

- Micro-manage – won't delegate projects, authority and responsibility to help people develop.
- Have a temper – get angry and abusive with people.
- Always know best – pretend to listen then ignore suggestions, belittle other people's ideas or just give orders.
- Fail to follow through on commitments – agree a course of action, but then not deliver on their actions.
- Lie – happily tell untruths if it helps them get their way or avoid responsibility.
- Always come first - insist that everything has to stop to deal with their priorities.
- Find fault – blame other people for failures.
- Provide no support – do not help other people to succeed.
- Act selfishly, with no concern for the effect of their demands on other people's lives.

2. What are the good points about this person? It is important to objectively focus on the actual behaviours, not just your negative perception of the person. This is because once we have formed a negative perception of someone, that is all we want to see. Then we look for further examples to support our negative opinion.

3. What part are you playing in the problem? Are you not pulling your weight? Are there performance or activity reasons why your boss might justifiably have an issue with your behaviour and therefore respond in ways that you consider toxic, but they consider reasonable in the circumstances?

4. If you have the misfortune to work for a toxic boss and are clear that you are not making the situation worse, what can you do? It's likely you'll need support. Who can you talk to within the company: HR, a director, a colleague? What about the Employee Assistance Programme helpline, if your employer subscribes to one? Can you discuss the issues directly with this toxic person, letting them know what they do, how that makes you feel and how you'd prefer them to behave?

Part
3

What I do

Manage the political landscape

I frequently hear Young Professionals say that they don't want to get involved in office politics, and therefore keep themselves to themselves. When politics means people arguing and nasty undercurrents, I completely understand why you would not want to get involved.

However, if you want an outstanding career, you cannot completely ignore politics. By its very nature as a collection of people, any organisation is a political structure. If you are going to be influential, you need to understand the political landscape and work it.

Think of politics as a play being acted out on the stage. If you're going to get anything from the viewing, you want to know what the plot is and the parts the actors are playing. Most plots involve a complex and diverse structure with dependencies, coalitions, co-operation and competition taking place. This is the political landscape.

The actors are the people playing their part within the landscape. There are stakeholders, decision-makers and influencers, all of whom are crucial actors. There is also the Inner Circle, the critical few people who make the really key decisions.

If you are going to build your reputation, you need to know who has the power and influence. These power brokers and influencers have the potential to be either strong supporters of your work, or to block it.

Crucial actors are:

- Stakeholders – individuals who have an interest in the area you work within and who get involved.
- Decision-makers – key individuals who hold the informal authority and resources to make things happen. Consider how they think, what motivates them and how you can get them interested in your work.
- Influencers – individuals who are well connected and rated by decision-makers. They are often trusted because of their strong record of successful delivery in the past.
- Inner circle – the critical few who really shape decisions and resource allocation.

A Political Landscape Map (sometimes called an Influence Map) is a visual model showing the crucial actors and the strength of their influence. It is useful because it will help you to identify the key people who you can influence and their interacting relationships. Your aim should be to broaden your network to include these people and build positive relationships with them, based on trust and respect, so that your ideas have credibility.

The benefits of doing this are:

- You can use the opinions of the most powerful crucial actors to shape your activities and tasks at an early stage. Not only does this make it more likely that they will support you, their input can also improve the quality of your work.
- Gaining support from these actors can help you to work on more impactful projects and tasks and become recognised as a person who can be trusted to deliver.
- By communicating with the right actors early and often, you can ensure that they know what you are doing and fully understand the value you bring. This means they can support you actively when necessary.
- You can anticipate what people's reaction to your work may be, and build into your plan the actions that will win people's support.

Part

3

What I do

Activity: Your political landscape

1. Take a piece of paper. Brainstorm the names of the crucial actors. Think of all the people who are affected by your work, who have influence or power over it or have an interest in its successful or unsuccessful conclusion. Remember that these are not necessarily people in your direct reporting line. You may therefore need to think outside your department/division (the use of organisational charts will assist you) and even outside of your employer.

2. Identify whether they are:

   - Stakeholders
   - Decision-makers
   - Influencers
   - Inner Circle

3. Identify the relationships between them by drawing lines between people. Use heavier lines where there is greater influence and arrows to show the direction of influence if it is one-way.

4. Identify the primary groups and coalitions. Draw circles around crucial actors to illustrate a group. Consider the following:

   - Which group is the Inner Circle?
   - Who is in each group?
   - Do the groups overlap?
   - How large and how tightly knit is each group?
   - Are there divisions/conflict between them?
   - Who is left out of a group?

5. Colour code your map to show who you expect to be an advocate or supporter for you, and who is likely to be a blocker or critic. (Advocates and supporters in green, blockers and critics in red, and others who are neutral in orange).

6. Use this map to help you work out how you become noticed and more influential.

   - Which relationships do you need to foster?
   - Who could help and support you, perhaps as a sponsor or mentor?
   - Who do you need to work more closely with to change their perceptions of you, your current contribution and your future potential?

7. To put this into practice, ensure that you understand more about them. A good way is to talk to them directly! Key questions that can help you understand your crucial actors are:

   - What financial or emotional interest do they have in the outcome of your work? Is it positive or negative?
   - What motivates them most of all?
   - What information do they want from you?
   - How do they want to receive information from you? What is the best way of communicating your message to them?

- What is their current opinion of your work? Is it based on good information?
- Who influences their opinions generally, and who influences their opinion of you? Do some of these influencers therefore become important stakeholders in their own right?
- Who else might be influenced by their opinions? Are these people stakeholders in their own right?

Remember that people and organisations change. Ensure you review and update your map after every significant change in the organisation or in its activities.

Activity: Your reflections

It is time again to reflect on your thoughts and the activities you have completed in this chapter.

Review the chapter in light of the following questions and record your answers below:

- What have you learned about yourself in this chapter?
- What do you need to change?
- What do you need to start doing that you have not done before?
- What other thoughts do you have?

9: My propeller to success

- Do you struggle to know who to contact when you need information outside your office?
- Do you get annoyed that you never seem to know what's going on in the company?
- Are you only interested in what's going on in your team?
- Do you try to keep your head down and hope that you won't get embroiled in a change activity?
- Do you rely on your annual review to discuss your career with your manager?

If the answer to any of these is Yes, then you need to pay special attention to this chapter.

So far, this book has shown you how self-awareness, career capital and reputation are the foundations of building a resilient career. However, if you want to really turbo-charge your career, you are going to need to get out there and be seen.

This means not just knowing what assets you have in your career capital fund, but actively seeking ways to grow these assets further. It means not just making your existing working relationships work more effectively, but broadening your portfolio of relationships so more people get to know you and your reputation. It means not just keeping your ears and eyes open to opportunities to enhance your knowledge but also using your voice to proactively find out more.

Case study

Ava was delighted when she got her new job in compliance. She'd thought for a long time that she was technically sound and this proved it.

She focused her activities on reviewing and developing processes and writing handbooks explaining how to operate in line with the regulatory requirements. Thank goodness she had her own office, because she could shut herself away and concentrate.

She was frequently asked to attend the monthly board meeting to report on what she was working on and how this would help to ensure the company was operating within the regulatory requirements. The day arrived when the company had a visit and review by the regulator. To Ava's complete surprise, it was an unmitigated disaster.

The regulator's inspectors identified an area of non-compliance with standards and put the company on warning. The CEO was furious with Ava. He had been humiliated and belittled by 'some young upstart' from the regulator for something he had not been warned could be an issue. The CEO couldn't understand why Ava hadn't known that this area was a hot topic with the regulator at the moment. What had he been paying her for?

What was happening here?

Ava was operating as a technical expert, relying on her existing knowledge. Her knowledge was good – but she had failed to take opportunities to grow it. There would have been a lot more to learn about regulations, how the regulators interpret the regulations and what they specifically look for when they undertake an inspection, if only Ava had asked the questions.

Attending forums and speaking to other compliance managers in the industry would have given her this invaluable information. The company could have ensured they had all areas covered, avoiding the embarrassment the CEO experienced.

Top tips to propel your career

1. Network, network, network. It's vital to enhance your career resilience. Networking is where you develop professional contacts. Employers adore people with good connections.

2. Take off the blinkers and develop a curiosity for the world. It all boils down to the power of asking questions.

3. Embrace change. This provides you with opportunities to learn and is a great way to build confidence.

4. Be on the lookout for every opportunity to leverage your career. Don't wait for the annual appraisal to discuss your ideas and aspirations. Take the initiative and negotiate. Whatever you do, don't take your eye off the end goal and stagnate.

Part
3

What I do

If you're going to have an outstanding career, you're going to have a network – there's no hiding from this.

Internal contacts – these are people within your firm who you can draw on at any time you need information, resources or access to others.

External contacts – these are gathered from actively going out and meeting people. This could mean attending or speaking at a conference, going to networking events held by your professional association or trade body, joining round-table forums as a representative of your company, offering your company as host for an event or simply approaching someone you admire in your industry (flattery always works). Employers love to hire people with connections, so developing an internal and an external network is a valuable asset in your career capital account.

A network takes time to develop but it's a powerful way to get your name out there and known in the business world. Not only will it grow your reputation, but also your influence, self-confidence and self-esteem.

The trick is to collect contact details whenever you meet someone new. Do not be shy or embarrassed asking for this. All successful business people do it. Do not limit your network just to people you are friends with or already have a business relationship with. Look beyond these to anyone you have made even the briefest acquaintance with at a meeting, or with a customer, or a professional contact, or an industry specialist. Think of it as throwing out a net to the people that work in your industry.

Activity: Your valuable network

Where do you keep your network of contacts? If you answered 'on my phone' - what would happen if you lost it? Is it backed up? If you answered 'on LinkedIn', how does that help you access the right person you need in that moment? Do you know how to use it effectively?

To use your network to the full, you need to know who you have, how valuable they really are and who you should be targeting.

1. Write down the names of all the contacts you have and the value they bring to your network
2. How diverse is your network? Remember it is a net which not only travels sideways but also up and down.
3. What areas of your business world are not yet represented? What do you need to do to populate your network with valuable people?
4. How could you make better use of your network?

Curiosity for the world

I so often hear from business leaders, "I want my professionals to have a curiosity for the world,"- but what does this actually mean?

Simply put - come out of the comfort zone that is your role and the team you work with and take an interest in the broader organisation and industry. It's about gaining knowledge: professional knowledge, company knowledge, competitor knowledge, industry knowledge – any knowledge. It all boils down to asking questions.

Children are curious and ask lots of questions; they are like sponges. Sadly, as soon as they start school they tend to lose the capacity for curiosity. Maybe it comes from the teacher's need to keep thirty boisterous children quiet and under control; but it's still a shame that this characteristic is lost.

Re-igniting your curiosity gives you a real edge. Business leaders tell me time and time again that they can identify Young Professionals with high potential very early on. They are the ones asking lots of questions.

Questions get you noticed because asking them shows your mind is open.

Questions demonstrate that you're inquisitive, interested, enthusiastic and open to new experiences.

Questions provide a learning opportunity that others won't necessarily get, putting you ahead of the competition.

Finally, questions make you more creative because they provide you with choices. This makes you powerful in a situation of change.

Activity: They know/you don't

Think back to the start of this book and at the various combinations of what you know and what you don't.

Here are some key things you need to know. Work out who currently holds this knowledge - then ask them, so that you can begin to populate the empty boxes.

Topic	What you know about this topic?
The company's plans for the next 5 years	
The cultural norms in the company – values, behaviours	
How my manager expects us to work together	

Part

3

What I do

Topic	What you know about this topic?
How my manager sees my career progressing within this company	
Opportunities within other parts of the organisation	
What customers really want	
Professional ethics and codes of practice	

Embrace change

There's one thing you can be sure of in the business world today and that's change. As a Young Professional, to be outstanding you need to embrace change, keep abreast of potential change and drive change yourself.

Do this and you will fly. People who embrace change show confidence, optimism, open-mindedness, creativity, flexibility and adaptability, all of which makes them resilient.

Change can present itself from anywhere and at any time. It could be a key member of your team leaving, or a new process being rolled out in your department. It could be a change in the ownership of your employer or a change in your profession, such as amalgamating with another professional body. It could be a change in law or a change of government. It's everywhere and no one is immune – so use it to its full advantage.

Part
3

What I do

Activity: My response to change

Think back to the last time you were told about a change that was in the pipeline.

* How did hearing that news make you feel?
* What did you do in response to that news?
* How would you approach that news now?
* What would happen to you if there was no change?

Keep growing to flourish

Throughout this book, I have advocated the necessity to find ways to develop your expertise and knowledge. This is because a resilient career is one that continues to grow. It is never a static place to be.

Develop and you will flourish. Snooze and be complacent, and you will stagnate. This will leave you frustrated, unhappy and dissatisfied with your working life. On-going development can be easier said than done because there are many barriers along the Young Professional's career journey.

1. **Too many demands:** As the demands and complexities of your role grow, so it will become harder to find the time and headspace to plan and seek out development opportunities. This is particularly the case if you are a Young Professional in your late twenties or early thirties.

2. **Autonomy:** Young Professionals are always telling me that they want more autonomy. Although this comes as your career develops, strangely, too much of it can hijack your development.

   Here's why: autonomy means being trusted and empowered to work independently, the way you want to work, and to make decisions. Since autonomy is one of the elements of wellbeing, it's no wonder it is held in such high esteem. However, if you want a resilient career, you need to treat autonomy with caution. If you allow yourself to work too independently, you risk becoming so embroiled in doing the job on your own that you become out of touch with opportunities to develop your capabilities. If you want autonomy, ensure you position it as a development opportunity where you can have a degree of independence and rather than being micro-managed, continue to be supported.

3. **Eye on the next job:** If you treat your career simply like a ladder to climb, you will eventually get to the top with nowhere else to go. This is because by focusing on finding and moving jobs, you have not given sufficient thought and effort to developing your knowledge and competence.

4. **Boredom:** If you are bored with work, there is every chance that this is because either you are not using your strengths or you have allowed your strengths to weaken because you have lost interest or failed to keep up with the industry.

Activity: Your stage of development

Have a look at the chart below. It shows the possible positions you could find yourself in as a Young Professional. Highlight the zone you are currently in.

	Getting bored with it	Experienced and performing well
High capability	Your level of competence is high but you're beginning to lose interest and passion in your work Zone 3	You're doing well, you're motivated and working to a high level of competence Zone 2
Low capability	**Stagnation** It's awful, you've started to fall behind on your capabilities and you have lost all motivation for your work Zone 4	**New to a job or project** You're keen and energised but you still have a lot to learn and skills to develop Zone 1
	Low motivation	High motivation

Part

3

What I do

Ask yourself the following:

- If you are in zone 1, what do you need to do to grow your capabilities?
- If you are in zone 2, what do you need to do to maintain your capabilities and motivation. You cannot stop just because you think you are there!
- If you are in zone 3, what do you need to do to fire up your motivation again? How can you make sure your capabilities do not lose their edge?
- If you are in zone 4, what do you need to do to get yourself back on track? This is not going to be easy because deep in this zone, you will feel stressed, demotivated and unhappy.

Propelling your career forward means continuous growth, so the best place to park yourself is zone 1.

Now you need to give some in-depth thought to what the barriers are to your career development. Identify these from the list below and add anything that has not been included but is relevant to you.

Business World	Organisation	Self
Political climate	Change programmes such as mergers and reorganisation	Personal limitations such as fear of rejection, indecisive, fear of change, low motivation, pessimism, low confidence
Technological change		
Industry transformation	Change in strategic direction	
Regulations and laws	Company culture	
Social pressures	Rules and procedures	Changes in personal life such as breakups, bereavement
The economy	Change in management - line manager/senior leadership	
Government changes		
		Financial pressures
Trade agreements	No promotion prospects	Living in the wrong location for the best jobs
Uncertainty		
Low demand for your skills	Lack of development opportunities	Responsibilities outside of work
	Pay below the market rate	Health/energy issues
	Strong competition from other employees	Lack of information
		Poor connections (networking)
	Discrimination	
	Unsupportive manager	Insufficient experience
		Lacking skills and/or essential qualifications

You do not have to do career development all on your own, although you do need to own it. Ask yourself, who can you help you?

Who can help?	How will you arrange it?
Manager: The person you report to. In the modern world, they no longer automatically look at ways you can advance your career. You need to negotiate a career deal with them, highlighting the value you can bring to the company.	
Coach: Someone either internal or external to the organisation who works with you to get you to find the answers.	
Mentor: Someone more senior and experienced in the company who can meet regularly to offer knowledge, advice and guidance and in so doing, inspire you.	

Part
3

What I do

Who can help?	How will you arrange it?
Sponsor: Someone who sees something special in you, so champions your progression.	
Role model: Someone you pick out who you would like to emulate. You don't have to meet them, but you read about them and watch them, picking up tips on what you could copy.	
Network: Your professional contacts inside and outside your organisation.	

Activity: Your reflections

It is time again to reflect on your thoughts and the activities you have completed in this chapter.

Review the chapter in light of the following questions and record your answers below:

- What have you learned about yourself in this chapter?
- What are you missing?
- What do you need to change?
- What do you need to start doing that you have not done before?
- What other thoughts do you have?

Part 4
Taking your career forward

10: Moving to action

To achieve that outstanding career, you'll need career resilience. Career resilience is founded on who you are, what you think and what you do. In all these ways, you need to stand out from the crowd of other Young Professionals and achieve your career aspirations. This means putting any fear you may have behind you, coming out of your comfort zone and taking responsibility for driving your career.

Sounds scary? Well - yes, but this chapter is here to guide you. It will gather up everything you have learned from this book so far and convert it into a plan of action: a plan of action that will create activities that embed themselves into the very way you function. This will create a way of life that will eventually become second nature to you – particularly when you see the benefits it brings to your career and wellbeing.

These activities will grow your capabilities and knowledge, enhance your reputation and influence, and convince whoever you work for, and whoever you come into contact with in your professional world, that you are of incredible value. It will make you eminently marketable.

You will be exploring your career aspirations, taking stock of where you are now and where you want to be. Combined with the reflections you made at the close of each chapter, you will create a plan of action.

This plan allows you to set some objectives and identify what you need to do to achieve them. Finally (and this is the exciting bit) you will explore just how you are going to get your employer to buy into this and support you.

Your vision

It is only by knowing what you want to achieve that you can create the activities that will get you there. With so many choices, this means that you will need to concentrate your efforts on only the capabilities, knowledge and actions that will give you the best result. Your vision is what will motivate you and provide you with the energy to see it though.

Activity: Your vision board

You already have an idea about what you want your career to look like. Now is the time to clearly define your aspirations in as much detail as possible, then come up with a plan to help you achieve it.

This is an exercise to conceptualise your vision and format it in a way that motivates you to work towards it and achieve it. A vision board is a collage of images, pictures, quotes and affirmations that create a visual representation of your dreams, goals, and the things that create a sense of professional success and happiness. The material can come from anywhere: magazines, the internet, books, photographs… anything that represents what you are trying to illustrate.

1. What is your vision? When you think about your career, what is it that you want to aspire to? Some of the following questions may help:

   a. Who do you want to become in your professional life?
   b. If nothing stood in your way, what would you want to achieve in your professional life?
   c. What does success look like – picture it.
   d. What would you like to be doing in five years time, ten years time and so on?
   e. How will this make you feel - what will it give you?
   f. When someone is delivering that speech at your retirement party, what accomplishments would you like them to be telling people about?
   g. Think about people you admire. What have they achieved that you would like to emulate?

2. Creating your vision board.

   a. What format for your board would suit you best? Ideas include a large piece of card, Pinterest, a web page, blog, or just a folder on your computer. Whatever it is, it must be easily accessible and somewhere you'd think to go to daily to view and update.

   b. Source inspiring pictures, words, quotes, sayings, and photos of people, including role models, that represent your vision. Good sources are the internet, magazines, newspapers, photographs and postcards.

   c. Choose the background you feel best suits your vision board. Is it patterned? What colour is it?

   d. What about the layout? Is it one big picture or divided into sections? Do you want only pictures or all words (such as a poem) or perhaps a bit of both?

   e. Now create your board!

Part

4

Taking your career forward

3. Your board is the visual reminder of what you want your career to be like. Once you have created the board, display it somewhere you will see it regularly. This engages your brain to seek out opportunities that help you achieve your desired outcomes.

4. Each time you see it, spend a while reflecting on what it is telling you and the progress you are making. Talk to yourself positively about it and create some positive affirmations/intentions based upon it, starting with "I will be...."

5. Regularly ask yourself whether it requires some updating. Visions are not cast in stone, stuff happens and life takes all sorts of twists and turns. Visions require an element of flexibility.

Your career platforms

1. Where are you and your career right now?

Before you can plan what you need to do to realise your vision, you need to take stock of the current state of your career. You've already begun this process with the reflections at the end of each chapter.

Activity: Your current career profile

This is your opportunity to benchmark your career as you move forward with your resilient career development – first as a Young Professional, and then as a professional. Answer the following questions:

1. What is your current role?
2. Describe how your role contributes towards your career vision.

3. To what degree are you doing what you need to be doing to achieve your career vision?

Respond to these questions based on what is happening right now. Score each question between 1 and 10 where 1 = low/very poor and where 10 = high/excellent

	Score
To what degree is your current role contributing to your vision?	
How do you feel about your career right now?	
How marketable would you consider yourself right now?	
How self-aware are you?	
How in control are you of your emotions?	
How much do you care for your physical and mental health?	
How valuable is your current career capital account to achieving your career vision?	
What is the current state of your reputation in your company/industry? When thinking about this, also include your level of visibility, influence and impact as these feed your reputation	
How strong are the relationships you have at work?	
How broad is your network?	
How open are you to change?	
How active are you at developing your career?	
What part/involvement does your employer play/have in your career?	

Part

4

Taking your career forward

2. What do you need to do?

It is time to summarise the reflections you made at the end of each chapter in the book and identify the activities required to fulfil your vision.

1. Look back over each reflection exercise you have completed.
2. In the right-hand column, record the actions you need to take to improve this element.

These actions need to move you out of your comfort zone, but should not be so challenging that they demotivate you so that you end up stagnating.

What did I learn?	What do I need to do?
Chapter 2: What is career resilience? Your life force, purpose, barriers to success, life balance	

What did I learn?	What do I need to do?
Chapter 3: Career Resilience Model	
Chapter 4: Self-awareness Purpose, self-concept, self-esteem and self-confidence	

Part

4

Taking your career forward

What did I learn?	What do I need to do?
Chapter 5: Self-control	
Chapter 6: Self-care Stress and organisation skills	

What did I learn?	What do I need to do?
Chapter 7: My career capital Competencies, qualities, training, qualifications, knowledge, relationships, experience, contacts, achievements and value	
Chapter 8: My reputation Personal brand, relationships, conflict and the political landscape	

Part

4

Taking your career forward

What did I learn?	What do I need to do?
Chapter 9: My propeller to success Networking, curiosity, embracing change and growth	

3. Looking through the list of actions you have written, identify and highlight your priorities.

4. Why will they make a difference to your career and enhance your career resilience?

5. How are you going to do it?

It's not about finding a new job, but how you can work in a new way within your current role. In other words, how you can craft your job into creating more career capital.

Whatever you do, make sure it increases the complexity of your tasks, grows your knowledge and competencies and raises your visibility in a clear and realistic way, otherwise it will do nothing for developing your career.

Consider the following:

a. What positive changes can you make to your existing role?
b. What can you add to your role, or even do as an extra?
c. What can you do in a different way that creates the space to add in something new?
d. What can you delegate to free up space and time?
e. What time can you allocate to develop your career?

6. Score your answers in order of priority. Priority is determined by what will grow your competence and enhance your reputation.

7. What extra resources do you need to help you?

8. If you prefer to make your goals SMART, then do so: make them Specific, Measurable, Achievable, Relevant and Timed.

Part

4

Taking your career forward

Action	How	Order of priority

9. Do you want or need help? If so who will help you? Think about your manager, a coach, mentor, sponsor, role model, and people in your network.

Who can help?	How will you arrange it?

Part

4

Taking your career forward

Activity: Your progress

You need to get into the habit of comparing yourself and your development with yourself, not comparing yourself with other people.

1. Write an email to yourself outlining the following:

   a. Your career vision.
   b. The role you play at work.
   c. The degree to which your current role contributes to you achieving your career vision. (For this, give yourself a score out of 10 where 0 is not at all and 10 is totally).
   d. What you want to have achieved for each of your priority objectives in the 6 months after writing this email.

2. Send the email to yourself. Put it in a career folder in your email box. Set a reminder to look at that email in six months' time.

3. In six months, reread the email and record your answers to the questions below in a reply email – this means you still have your original email in the body of this reply email:

   • What is your career vision? If it has changed, what is it now?
   • What progress have you made in the last six months towards achieving your vision?
   • How are you currently performing in your role? Score yourself again on the degree to which this contributes to you achieving your career vision. Give yourself a score out of 10 where 0 is 'not at all' and 10 is 'totally'.
   • How has your role changed in the last six months?
   • How much has your career grown in the last six months?
   • What are you doing differently that demonstrates this growth?
   • How have your competencies changed?
   • How has your reputation changed?
   • What feedback have you received?
   • Are you doing what you really want to do? If not, identify what you should be doing in the next six months.
   • What do you hope to achieve in the next six months?

4. Send the reply to yourself and store in your career folder. Set a reminder to review this email in six months time. Review what you said six months ago and continue the process of replying to the email using the questions recorded in 3 above.

5. By replying to each email including the body of the previous emails, you will create a diary that tracks your career progress. All you have to do is scroll down through the email to see how far you have come.

Get your employer on board

As we've discussed, employers no longer take responsibility for developing your career and progressing you up the career ladder. Today it's all down to you. Because you own your career, you must ensure that you are off autopilot and wide-awake, being proactive and making time for your own development.

It's helpful to think of yourself as a supplier to the organisation with a business proposition that adds value to them. This makes you indispensable, gives you marketability and sets you aside from your competitors.

Once you have prepared your career vision and plan, it's time to negotiate with your manager to get the collateral and support you require. Although your career is your responsibility, there is absolutely no reason why your employer cannot assist – you just need to demonstrate what's in it for them.

Be clear: this is not about a promotion or a pay rise. This is about creating a resilient career that generates success and wellbeing and makes you feel happy and satisfied. This in turn provides great benefits for the organisation.

Part

4

Taking your career forward

Activity: Your career negotiation

1. Give some thought to the career conversations you have had with your manager over the last two years. Review any appraisals and personal development plans you have. (Annual appraisals are always thought of as an ordeal by both parties so just use the information generated: do not try to replicate the process).

2. Decide who you would like to have a meeting with about your career. This could be your manager, HR or maybe your sponsor. Your manager is preferable.

3. Prepare for the meeting by creating a proposal document covering the following:

   a. Your career vision.
   b. Your career capital, what you offer the company and the advantages to them in employing you. Demonstrate your loyalty, your worth and what makes you unique in the current market.
   c. What do you need to do to achieve your vision? (It's helpful to sort these into one, three and five year time-frames).
   d. What would you like the company to do and how much will it cost?
   e. What are the business benefits to the organisation if they support you? Will it generate more income, increase their visibility or market share?

4. Set up a meeting and send out your proposal document in advance of the meeting.

5. Come organised and prepared. Perhaps an agenda will help you stay on track.

6. Introduce the purpose of the session and the roles each of you will play. You need to take charge and own this meeting.

7. You are seeking opportunities that will enhance your capabilities so allow your manager (or whoever this discussion is with) to help you to explore and identify what you could do and the resources available to assist you. Accept as learning any feedback offered. If it is negative, do not take it personally but explore in the meeting how you will overcome this.

8. Ask questions.

9. Hold a meeting like this regularly. More and more companies are moving away from the annual appraisal and towards regular real-time feedback. If your company does not provide it, ask for it.

    If your manager is unresponsive, then this is a hurdle you need to overcome. Go back to the planning stage and plan for negotiating your development in a new way. Whatever you do, do not give up.

    Lack of response from your manager may mean you have to finance everything yourself or work on your career development during non-work times such as weekends. If you look on this as an investment (because you cannot progress without it), the rewards will be sweet when they come in.

Part

4

Taking your career forward

11: And to support you...

I hope you have enjoyed this book and found it of immense value to you and your career.

I'm sure at times it has challenged you, but managing a career is challenging by its very nature. Overcoming challenges takes us out of our comfort zone and opens up a whole new world to us. It ignites our capacity to grow and become more resilient and successful.

With such a vast topic, there is only so much room for explanation. If you require any further information or tips on how to have an outstanding career, then go to our website at www.youngprofs.net.

Let us know how you get on. Stories of transformation are always of great interest to me. It's real people that bring careers alive and I for one am still learning.

You can reach me at susan@youngprofs.net

We have two other forthcoming books in the series:

- The Young Professional's Guide to preventing burnout
- The Young Professional's Guide to optimising your personal energy.

Both are practical guides specialising in the self-care aspect of career resilience. They contain lots of theory and exercises you will not find in this book. Go to our website for further information.

To finish, here are some top tips for creating a resilient career. Despite the ever-changing and volatile world we live and work in, we can still establish resilient careers by paying attention to and taking action over the following;

- Always be curious – it's a rare gift today, but a big distinguishing factor.

- Take the initiative – if you don't, someone else will.

- Seize the moment to act – remain awake. There's plenty of time to sleep when you retire!

- Embrace change.

- Grow your strengths and generate visibility for them – think projects, blogs, presentations.

- Ask everyone for feedback, and act on it.

- Always have your personal brand pitch at the forefront of your mind.

- Show determination to deliver and take ownership of the outcomes – people will respect you for it.

- Know the key players in the organisation, and industry and play them.

- Focus on on-going self-growth and development – you can't afford to stagnate.

- Always be learning – knowledge is power.

- Network, network, network – it's a must.

- Appreciate and accept your feelings – be positive whilst acknowledging the negative for what it is.

- Accept that resilience may mean focusing on things that help us achieve our longer-term goals rather than the things that deliver short term pleasure.

- Realise that we often cannot change the situation, but we can change how we think and feel about it and then figure out your plan of action.

- Have a mentor or coach – even if you pay for it yourself, it will reap immeasurable benefits.

- Stay healthy and recognise your stress triggers and how you react.

- Be your own person – don't try to be or compare yourself with anyone but yourself. You're a powerful, effective, dynamic Young Professional.

Part

4

Taking your career forward

Lightning Source UK Ltd.
Milton Keynes UK
UKOW05f0905030517
300372UK00002B/151/P